Introducing Business English

Introducing Business English provides a comprehensive overview of this topic, situating the concepts of Business English and English for Specific Business Purposes within the wider field of English for Special Purposes. This book draws on contemporary teaching and research contexts to demonstrate the growing importance of English within international business communication.

Covering both spoken and written aspects of Business English, this book:

- examines key topics within Business English, teaching Business English as a Lingua Franca, intercultural business interactions, blended learning and web-based communication;
- discusses the latest research on each topic, and possible future directions;
- features tasks and practical examples, a section on course design, and further resources.

Written by two leading researchers and teachers, *Introducing Business English* is a must-read for advanced undergraduate and postgraduate students studying Business English, Business English as a Lingua Franca, and English for Specific Business Purposes.

Catherine Nickerson is a professor in the College of Business at Zayed University in the United Arab Emirates. Her research focuses on Business English and the use of English as a Lingua Franca in business contexts.

Brigitte Planken is an associate professor at the Department of Communication and Information Studies and a researcher at the Centre for Language Studies, Radboud University Nijmegen, the Netherlands. She has published widely on Business English, language policy in organizations, and corporate communication.

Routledge Introductions to English for Specific Purposes provide a comprehensive and contemporary overview of various topics within the area of English for specific purposes, written by leading academics in the field. Aimed at postgraduate students in applied linguistics, English language teaching and TESOL, as well as pre- and in-service teachers, these books outline the issues that are central to understanding and teaching English for specific purposes, and provide examples of innovative classroom tasks and techniques for teachers to draw on in their professional practice.

SERIES EDITOR: BRIAN PALTRIDGE

Brian Paltridge is Professor of TESOL at the University of Sydney. He has taught English as a second language in Australia, New Zealand and Italy and has published extensively in the areas of academic writing, discourse analysis and research methods. He is editor emeritus for the journal *English for Specific Purposes* and has co-edited the *Handbook of English for Specific Purposes* (Wiley, 2013).

SERIES EDITOR: SUE STARFIELD

Sue Starfield is Associate Professor in the School of Education and Director of The Learning Centre at the University of New South Wales. Her research and publications include tertiary academic literacies, doctoral writing, writing for publication, identity in academic writing and ethnographic research methods. She is a former editor of the journal *English for Specific Purposes* and co-editor of the *Handbook of English for Specific Purposes* (Wiley, 2013).

TITLES IN THIS SERIES

Introducing Business English
Catherine Nickerson and Brigitte Planken

Introducing English for Academic Purposes
Maggie Charles and Diane Pecorari

Introducing Needs Analysis and English for Specific Purposes
James Dean Brown

Introducing Genre and English for Specific Purposes
Sunny Hyon

Introducing English for Specific Purposes
Laurence Anthony

Introducing Course Design and English for Specific Purposes
Lindy Woodrow

Introducing Business English

Catherine Nickerson and
Brigitte Planken

Routledge
Taylor & Francis Group

LONDON AND NEW YORK

First published 2016
by Routledge
2 Park Square, Milton Park, Abingdon, Oxon OX14 4RN

and by Routledge
711 Third Avenue, New York, NY 10017

Routledge is an imprint of the Taylor & Francis Group, an informa business

British Library Cataloguing-in-Publication Data
A catalogue record for this book is available from the British Library

Library of Congress Cataloging in Publication Data
Nickerson, Catherine, 1965-
Introducing business English / Catherine Nickerson and Brigitte Planken.
pages cm. -- (Routledge introductions to english for specific purposes)
Includes bibliographical references and index.
1. English language--Business English--Study and teaching. 2. Business communication--Study and teaching. I. Planken, Brigitte Chantal, 1966- II. Title.
PE1479.B87N53 2015
808.06'665--dc23
2015021308

ISBN: 978-1-138-01627-9 (hbk)
ISBN: 978-1-138-01631-6 (pbk)
ISBN: 978-1-315-69433-7 (ebk)

Typeset in Sabon
by Taylor & Francis Books

For all our students

Contents

Part I

Introduction

Part I.

Introduction

Chapter 1

What is Business English?

Introduction

This chapter introduces Business English and English for Specific Purposes and explains how they have developed and influenced the teaching of Business English over the past two decades. It also introduces some of the scholars who have been most influential in the field of Business English, explains how their work has helped shape that field and discusses the implications their work has had for the teaching of Business English. Next, the chapter highlights the importance of the interconnections between written texts and spoken forms of communication and shows that this interrelatedness is typical of how English is used in the contemporary business context. In doing so, it introduces the terms *intertextuality* and *interdiscursivity* and explains how these have been referred to in research. Finally, the chapter provides readers with an overview of the rest of the book.

In this book, we use Business English as an umbrella term to refer to any interaction, written or spoken, that takes place in English, where the purpose of that interaction is to conduct business. For example, it can be used to refer to a business meeting, an email sent to set up a business appointment, or an advertisement promoting a new product. All of these events or documents have been studied by researchers with an interest in Business English and they are also all likely to be included or referred to in a Business English training course. We will see that the focus on different – and discrete – genres, i.e. on different types of spoken and written Business English and their distinctive characteristics (in terms of their content, structure, and goal), has been a common feature of studies of Business English, and of investigations of written Business English in particular. We explore this in Part II for spoken Business English and in Part III for written Business English.

As we discuss in more detail in the next chapter, Business English is different to most other languages used to conduct business because nowadays so many people in so many different parts of the world use it as a communication 'code' to facilitate their work. While other languages like Mandarin Chinese (Putonghua), Hindi, and Spanish are used by many business people in specific geographical locations, Business English has a special status because it is used by such large numbers of native speakers, second language speakers, and foreign language speakers across the globe regardless of their location or first language, and also in situations where those speakers are frequently in interaction with each other, both virtually and face-to-face. As a result, in many places Business English co-exists alongside one or more other languages used in business, and the business people that use it may switch between English and their own first or additional languages. As we discuss in more detail in the next chapter, Business English is now often viewed as a necessary skill for succeeding in business, just as having good computer skills or an understanding of accounting might be required.

The teaching of Business English has been strongly connected to the research field of English for Specific Purposes for more than three decades, and more specifically since the publication of Johns' (1980) landmark publication 'Cohesion in written business discourse' published in the inaugural issue of the *ESP Journal*, now *English for Specific Purposes*. This publication, which looked at the language items that occurred together in letters, reports, and business textbooks – i.e. the 'constellations' of cohesive items – marked the beginning of research into Business English as a prominent area of interest within English for Specific Purposes.

Johns found that there were differences in the language items that occurred together in each of the three types of documents that she looked at, and research like this – looking for both similarities and differences in different types of communication used for business – has continued to be a common feature of English for Specific Purposes research since that time. Johns' article also made an important distinction between applied Business English (as represented at that time by business letters and reports), and academic English for business and economics (as represented by business textbooks). Researchers interested in Business English have also often focused on either applied Business English or on academic Business English. This book is about applied Business English and the different forms of communication that have evolved and been studied since the publication of Johns' article.

In Task 1.1, you are asked to characterize forms of communication that are common in today's workplace.

Task 1.1 Communication at work: the context for Business English

While research has shown that email has become increasingly important in today's business world, business people – and companies – have at their disposal many other forms of communication, such as letters or websites, which are used to communicate both internally (e.g. with colleagues) and externally .g. with clients or consumers).

First, list at least three different forms of communication besides email that employees might use in the workplace.

Next, think of a specific business situation or business task in which each form might be used, and identify the purpose and the audience.

Then, within the context of the business situation or task you have identified for each form of communication, characterize it in terms of whether it is written or spoken, virtual or real-time, personal or corporate, internal or external, one-way or two-way, face-to-face or long-distance, informative or persuasive.

Finally, consider which type(s) of communication should be dealt with in a Business English course, and give reasons why you think this is important.

A second important article that has helped to shape the field of Business English was published by Williams in *Applied Linguistics* (Williams, 1988). Williams investigated the language used in three meetings by 12 native speakers of English and compared this with the language that was used in 30 English textbooks aimed at teaching people Business English for meetings. She found that there were very few similarities between the real language used in business meetings and the model language presented in the textbooks to learners, as the language used by real speakers was much more complicated than the language presented in the textbooks. Williams' study has continued to be influential because it highlighted the mismatch that can exist between teaching materials and real language. In the decades since the study was published, other researchers have carried out similar studies (e.g. St John, 1996; Nickerson, 2005). These studies have shown that a mismatch continues to exist in many of the published textbooks that are intended to teach Business English. Later in this book, we look at some of the Business English textbooks that have incorporated real language, embedded in real business tasks, into the models and exercises they present.

Johns' and Williams' studies encapsulate many of the continuing concerns of Business English and English for Specific Purposes research that focuses on business interactions and texts. English for Specific Purposes is mainly concerned with two things: first, the collection and analysis of real data, including extra contextual information on how that data is used by business people, and second, the application of the research findings in a classroom setting in order to maximize the effectiveness of teaching a specific form of communication. English for Specific Purposes is both descriptive, in that it tries to uncover or deconstruct the characteristics of a particular form of communication, and prescriptive, in that it uses real data and empirical analysis to make suggestions about how best to teach or train people to communicate effectively in a specific context. Researchers with an interest in Business English are often also active as teachers or trainers, and it is characteristic of the field that they have frequently drawn on both the descriptive and prescriptive nature of English for Specific Purposes in their research publications. In the next section, we describe three studies of Business English that were motivated by pedagogy – i.e. in order to design an appropriate set of teaching or training materials. One took place in Hong Kong (Li So-mui & Mead, 2000), one in a Finnish multinational operating in various countries around the world (Charles & Marschan-Piekkari, 2002), and one in the call centre industry in Asia (Lockwood, 2012). These studies are illustrative of the close connection between Business English and the research approach inherent in English for Specific Purposes. For each study, we outline what the researchers did and how their findings can be used to design an appropriate teaching programme.

Task 1.2 Comparing real-life and textbook data

Go to the library and borrow a prescriptive textbook on business communication that includes samples – in English – of business letters or business emails (e.g. letters of complaint or request emails).

Next, for one type of sample text you have found in the textbook, find some authentic, real-life examples of the same text type. These might be actual letters or emails in English written by you, your friends, family, or colleagues. Two to five texts of each type (textbook examples and real-life letters) should be sufficient for the task.

Compare the two sets of texts in terms of at least the following aspects:

- structure
- level of formality
- salutation and closing
- English (grammar, syntax, spelling, vocabulary, punctuation, etc.).

What similarities and differences did you notice between the two sets of texts?
  Where do the two sets of texts differ most?
  Do you think any of the differences you identified in the authentic texts (versus the textbook texts) would impede the effectiveness of the communication? In what way?
  Based on your comparison, what do you think deserves attention in a Business English course? Explain your answers.

Three studies of Business English

Li So-mui and Mead's (2000) study investigated the English needed by textile and clothing merchandisers in Hong Kong. The study details what is known as a *needs analysis* survey, which means an investigation aimed at collecting information in different ways to determine what a particular target group's needs are. In Li So-mui and Mead's study the aim was to find out what Hong Kong merchandisers needed to do with Business English at the time the study took place, and what they would need to do with Business English in the future, as the result of changes in the business environment, for example. The study was carried out specifically to develop learning and teaching materials for tertiary level institutions training textile merchandisers in Hong Kong.

Li So-mui and Mead used four information sources: 1) questionnaires completed by Hong Kong merchandisers, all of whom had had English or communication training, and all of whom had been working for at least one year, 2) follow-up telephone interviews with senior employees, 3) an analysis of a set of workplace texts considered typical of the sorts of texts that the merchandisers needed to deal with, and 4) a set of visits to the workplace to observe what the merchandisers did. The researchers were able to show that although more than half of the merchandisers used spoken English at work, English was in fact used much more for writing than it was for speaking. In addition, they were also able to identify the countries with whom the merchandisers were mostly doing business (mainland China, the United States, Japan, Taiwan, Korea, and Canada), the channels of communication they used (at that time – in the mid-nineties – fax and telephone), and why they needed to write (e.g. to describe products, to follow up an order, to clarify orders, etc.). The analysis of written documents also allowed them to identify a mismatch between the faxes presented in textbooks and the real fax texts that their respondents had to deal with. As in the study of business meetings by Williams (1988) discussed before, the textbook faxes were considerably less complex than the authentic faxes.

The information collected during this study allowed Li So-Mui and Mead to understand the ways in which Business English was used in the textile industry in Hong Kong, the skills that were most needed, the people textile merchandisers needed to be able to talk to, the channels they needed to focus on, and what tasks they needed to achieve with language. This in turn meant that the researchers could provide students studying merchandising with appropriate language learning activities to more effectively prepare them to deal with the Business English tasks that would be required of them in the future.

The study of the multinational corporation Kone Elevators by Charles and Marschan-Piekkari (2002), involved both an extensive interview survey and a set of more in-depth follow-up interviews. As in the case of Li So-Mui and Mead's study of the communication used by textile merchandisers, the aim was to design appropriate communication training for Kone Elevator employees working in middle management. Charles and Marschan-Piekkari held interviews with 110 staff located in ten different countries in Europe, Mexico, and the Far East. They followed these up with six in-depth interviews with key people (usually referred to as *key informants* in this type of study) within the organization. The researchers asked employees about their experiences with language and about any specific problems they encountered in which language had played a role. In addition, they asked the key informants about the history of language training at the corporation. The study is an example of a linguistic audit, which is an extensive and systematic needs analysis survey that not only identifies existing and future language needs, but also seeks to identify specific situations in which different languages either are or could be used, and the different forms of communication that are needed (or could be needed) in each one of those situations. A linguistic audit carried out in this way – that is, mapping languages, situations, and forms of communication – can identify new business opportunities, such as opportunities that are lost or ignored because employees need better Business English skills. We discuss the use of linguistic audits in more detail in Part V of this book.

Some of the recommendations in the Kone study were that listening comprehension was a very important skill that needed to be developed in addition to language production, and also that employees at Kone should be trained to become familiar with 'global Englishes' such as the English produced by Japanese, Dutch, French, and Indian speakers, so that they could deal with different accents, communication strategies, and expressions. We discuss this study in more detail in the next chapter when we look at the use of Business English as an international language and the role that native speakers play in international communication. Also, we discuss how its findings could be used in the design of an appropriate corporate training course.

Lockwood's (2012) study is focused on the call centre industry, specifically on a large call centre organization providing customer service with major offices in both India and the Philippines. Lockwood describes how she and her research team were tasked by the organization to provide a Business English training curriculum as well as an English language assessment strategy to be used in evaluating employees. The language assessment strategy was implemented first, followed by the training curriculum. As in the previous two studies that we have discussed here, the researchers used several different methods and consulted several different types of people to collect the information they needed to develop the assessment test and the curriculum. Their aim was to take the views and experiences of different types of employees or stakeholders into account, including the customer service representatives themselves, their account managers, and the human resource recruiters and trainers who would eventually be responsible for administering the assessment test and implementing the training curriculum. The research team conducted a communication audit which included recordings of a sample of customer service calls representing the different accounts in India and the Philippines and observations of customer service employees at work, together with focus group interviews with different stakeholders in the organization. A focus group interview is a structured interview with a small group of people who are likely to share similar work experience, interests, and concerns. In this study, for example, focus group discussions were held with recruitment personnel, trainers, and account managers.

The analysis of the sample customer service calls showed the researchers that newly employed customer service representatives would need to be able to deal with a range of different types of calls at different levels of complexity, ranging from relatively simple tasks such as changing a customer's postal address to more complex tasks such as chasing a credit card debt. The researchers tried to capture these different levels of difficulty by ranking the different calls that representatives might encounter from easy to difficult. This ranking could then be used to underpin the training course. The analysis of the calls also allowed the research team to identify what caused most problems during an interaction – things like understanding sarcasm or jokes or UK regional accents – and this again enabled them to make specific choices with regard to the focus of the training materials that they went on to develop.

In the end, a selection of ten authentic calls at different levels of complexity, exemplifying different problems encountered in interactions and providing both good and bad examples, was used as the basis for the training course. The training materials that were produced on the basis of each authentic call included a number of tasks that referred to topics such as listening comprehension, pronunciation, and intercultural awareness tasks. As was the case in the Kone Elevators study, the research team recommended that the emphasis in teaching should be on promoting global comprehensibility, and not on trying to get learners to reproduce native speaker-like language and accents.

The language assessment framework the team developed not only evaluated pronunciation, as had often been the case in the company before the research team was asked to intervene, but also included an evaluation of other areas such as interactional and strategic ability, which the analysis of the authentic calls had shown to be crucial skills. Above all, Lockwood's account shows the added value of referring to real data in using an English for Specific Purposes approach in the design of a highly specialized Business English training course.

Personal Reflection 1.1

1 Think of a recent telephone interaction you have had with a call centre representative.

   Were there any difficulties in the interaction?
   How would you describe these difficulties?
   What do you think caused them?

2 If you were asked to design a training course for call centre employees so that they could deal effectively with customers from your country, what would you focus on and what might you include?

   What information would you need to collect in order to design an appropriate course?
   What methods would you use to collect this information?

Business English around the world

People interested in research into Business English using an English for Specific Purposes approach are located across the globe. When the field was being established, many of the researchers and many of the texts that they investigated, such as the pioneering studies by Ann Johns (Johns, 1980) and Marian Williams (Williams, 1988), were focused on the Anglo-Saxon business world. Gradually, however, the focus has broadened, moving through contrastive studies that compared the Business English produced by non-native and native speakers – such as Sims and Guice (1992) on business letters, Nickerson (2000) on email, and Maier (1992) on politeness in business letters – to more recent studies that have focused on global business interactions. The emphasis in later studies, such as Planken (2005) on international negotiations and Poncini (2004) and Rogerson-Revell (2008) on multicultural business meetings, has been on the strategies used by both native and non-native speakers. We look in more detail at studies like these in Chapter 4.

In addition to the work of individual researchers and teachers, it is also possible to identify institutions that have specialized in teaching Business English in various parts of the world. In northern Europe, for instance, Aalto Business School at Aalto University in Helsinki in Finland has a team of researchers – Mirjaliisa Charles, Anne Kankaanranta, and Leena Louhiala-Salminen – who have been very influential in the development of Business English in the European context, particularly through their work on Business English as a Lingua Franca, which we discuss in more detail in the next chapter. They in turn have close connections with the Department of Communication and Information Studies at Radboud University Nijmegen in the Netherlands, and researchers like Brigitte Planken, Frank van Meurs, and Elizabeth de Groot. Both institutions specialize in international business communication and pursue a similar approach to the teaching and training needs of equivalent student populations. Outside Europe, the College of Business at Zayed University in the United Arab Emirates (UAE) has more recently developed an interest in teaching and researching Business English in the context of the Middle East, as exemplified in the work of Catherine Nickerson and Gina Poncini, both of whom come from the English for Specific Purposes tradition. In Asia, various institutions in Hong Kong have long had an interest in the English used by the professions, including Business English. Vijay Bhatia, for instance, spent many years at City University in Hong Kong and has been a major influence on the field, as we discuss in Part III of this book. Other researchers such as Bertha Du-Babcock, Jane Lockwood, and Stephen Bremner (all at City University) and Winnie Cheng, Stephen Evans, and Martin Warren (all at the Research Centre for Professional Communication in English at Hong Kong Polytechnic University) have contributed greatly to our understanding of various forms of applied Business English. We discuss their work on spoken and written genres of Business English in more detail in Parts II and III respectively.

The research on Business English curriculum assessment and Business English needs conducted within the Research Centre for Business English and Cross-Cultural Studies at the University of International Business and Economics (UIBE) in Beijing, China, has also expanded our knowledge of Business English practices and needs, with important implications for Business English teaching exemplified in the work of Zuocheng Zhang. Zhang's (2013) investigation of international business professionals' versus business students' expectations of various Business English writing genres uncovered differences between the genre knowledge that students are taught in courses, and the genre knowledge they actually need in order to produce Business English writing that meets employers' expectations in real-life workplace contexts. The discrepancies noted between the two groups of informants in the ways they dealt with aspects of business writing genres served to show "that a gap still exists between the class-room and the profession" (Zhang, 2013, p. 154). The findings of studies such as those conducted by the Business English Research Group at UIBE emphasize the usefulness of research-based curriculum development for English for Special Purposes in general, and for Business English programmes in particular (see also Zhang, 2007). Finally, at Victoria University of Wellington, New Zealand, the Language in the Workplace project has been running in the School of Linguistics and Applied Language Studies since 1996, as exemplified, for instance, in the work of Janet Holmes, Meredith Marra, and Bernadette Vine (see www.victoria.ac.nz/lals/centres-and-institutes/language-in-the-workplace). The project focuses on spoken communication in New Zealand workplaces and has generated both research work and training materials. We discuss the project in more detail in Part II of this book, as an example of how Business English researchers have become more interested in multicultural interactions in business over the course of the past two decades.

Interconnections in Business English

An important characteristic of applied Business English that has been high-lighted by researchers taking an English for Specific Purposes approach is the highly interconnected nature of the communication. For instance, an email message may refer to a previous email or to a previous or forthcoming meeting, while a business presentation may refer to previous business presentations or to other business events such as a business relationship or a business deal. The process through which one individual text (either spoken or written) refers to another individual text (either spoken or written) is called *intertextuality*. In more general terms, where one type or genre of text (either spoken or written) is used by writers or speakers to construct, support, or co-create another type of text (e.g. a regular meeting supported by memos and co-created by agendas and minutes), the term *interdiscursivity* is sometimes used to describe the process of interlinking discourses (Bhatia, 2010). In this book we will be using both *intertextuality* and *interdiscursivity* to describe the general and specific connections between different types of Business English texts, both written and spoken.

One of the first scholars to look at intertextuality in business texts was Devitt (1991), who considered three different types of connection in tax accounting texts. She distinguishes between *referential* intertextuality (the specific references across different texts), *functional* intertextuality (the creation of a network of texts by the tax accounting profession to facilitate their professional goals) and *generic* intertextuality (the similarities between the different types of texts that are recognized as similar by the members of the same profession). Other researchers have carried out similar work on other types of Business English texts. For example, Akar and Louhiala-Salminen (1999) looked at business faxes, Gimenez (2006) and Evans (2012) looked at emails, and Evans (2013) looked at business presentations. We will discuss intertextuality and interdiscursivity in more detail in Part IV of this book, including how this crucial element in Business English could be incorporated into the classroom.

The need for research-based teaching

Traditionally, Business English teachers readily used insights from English for Specific Purposes more generally, not only as a basis for establishing learners' needs, but also to inform their teaching approach and to develop curricula and teaching materials. In recent years, however, researchers and practitioners alike have come to recognize that Business English is a particular form of English for Specific Purposes, with its own content, discursive practices, community of practitioners and forms of communication or genres, and that it can therefore be regarded as "an independent field of interdisciplinary study" (Zhang, 2007, p. 409). A complementary source of inspiration for Business English teachers can therefore be found in the increasing number of studies by researchers of business communication that have investigated how professionals use English to do business in a globalized workplace. These studies have not only provided insights into the contextual and situational factors that shape and influence its use, but have also described the characteristics of Business English. Such studies have primarily aimed to provide insights into the discursive and professional practices of business people who use English for work in an international arena. However, a secondary but no less important purpose has been to understand what it means to communicate effectively to reach professional goals in the workplace. In doing so, these studies aim to "bridge the gap between the classroom and business" (Bhatia & Bremner, 2012, p. 411). Most recently, researchers interested in Business English have acknowledged that the need to cross this divide is especially urgent because English continues to grow as the lingua franca of international business, as we will see in the next chapter. In this book we will also explore how insights from business communication research can be incorporated into teaching in order to make course materials relevant for global learners of Business English.

Structure of the book

In the next chapter, we discuss the special role that English has played as a business lingua franca and an international business language. This concludes Part I. In Part II we look at spoken business discourse in detail, including the different forms of communication that are used in the business world, the impact of intercultural communication, and how the research that has been done in these areas can be used in the classroom. In Part III we provide a similar discussion for written business discourse, with information on how written Business English texts are produced and interpreted, and again how these can be incorporated into the classroom. In Part IV, we consider the modern business world, including the impact of new media and the intertextual and interdiscursive nature of Business English, with ideas for teaching materials and classroom activities. Finally, in Part V, we discuss learners, teachers, and materials in more detail, including how to deal with advanced or near-native levels of proficiency in Business English, how to incorporate approaches such as project-based learning and blended learning, and data collection methods such as a needs analysis survey or communication audit to help in planning appropriate curricula, materials, and tasks. The final chapter in the book is a resources chapter with a set of additional reading materials, together with information on other resources such as conferences and professional societies concerned with researching and teaching Business English.

Summary

In this chapter, we have defined the way in which the term Business English will be used throughout this book and discussed the special relationship between Business English and the approach to research known as English for Specific Purposes. We have talked about some of the most influential people in the field, some of the work that they have done and where they are located, and we have introduced the related terms intertextuality and interdiscursivity. Finally, we have provided an overview of the rest of the volume. In the next chapter, we examine the role played by Business English both as a lingua franca and as an international business language.

Chapter 2

International Business English and Business English as a Lingua Franca

Introduction

In Chapter 1, we introduced Business English as an umbrella term to refer to any written or spoken interaction that takes place in English where the purpose of that interaction is to conduct business. We also introduced English for Specific Purposes as an important research approach that has been used to investigate Business English interactions, specifically to contribute to and improve on the ways in which Business English is taught. In this chapter, we look in detail at the different groups of people that are involved in Business English interactions in contemporary business settings, and we define the terms *International Business English* and *Business English as a Lingua Franca* as specific types of Business English. We show how the study of International Business English and Business English as a Lingua Franca has become increasingly relevant for English for Specific Purposes, and also therefore for the development of appropriate Business English teaching materials.

Business English as a Lingua Franca interactions take place between people for whom English is a second (or additional) language, whereas International Business English interactions involve native speakers as well as non-native speakers of English. As we discuss later in this chapter, this distinction is important because Business English Lingua Franca interactions are sometimes more successful than International Business English interactions. English for Specific Purposes researchers who investigate English used for business have gradually turned their attention to Business English as a Lingua Franca and International Business English because they have realized that their research should also aim to provide greater insight into the relationship between the communication that takes place in Business English and the associated work-related tasks and activities. This in turn has led to an increasing interest in investigating the use of English in international and intercultural organizational contexts, because the influence of globalization has meant that many more business interactions now involve people who do not speak English as their first language. In a parallel development, most Business English scholars now believe that it is no longer necessary to refer exclusively to native-speaker models in teaching. As a result, researchers interested in Business English are now much more likely to focus on the use of English as a business lingua franca or international business language than on communication involving only native speakers.

We will also see that this emphasis on learning about actual business *practices* has meant that in recent years International Business English and Business English as a Lingua Franca studies have tended to approach Business English from the perspective of business discourse. Bargiela-Chiappini et al. (2013) note that researchers have become interested in "language as social action in business contexts" and have tried to find out more "about how people communicate using talk or writing in commercial organizations in order to get their work done" (p. 3). Because of this, the emphasis in research has moved from the mechanics of language in business situations to how business people interact in order to achieve their business goals. With its emphasis on understanding how discourse is used by professional people, including those in business, Vijay Bhatia's work in this area has been very influential. He has referred to this as the relationship between their discursive and professional practices (Bhatia, 2004). In addition, as many researchers interested in International Business English or Business English as a Lingua Franca are also active in Business English teaching, the methods traditionally associated with the study of Language for Specific Purposes and English for Specific Purposes that we discussed in Chapter 1, including needs analysis and genre analysis, have also been used in researching Business English, often in research designs that combine multiple methodologies (e.g. survey-based needs analysis with text analysis, interviews, or observation).

Overall, International Business English and Business English as a Lingua Franca research that has taken a discourse approach has been mainly concerned with bridging the gap between teaching and professional practice. That is, it has been concerned with understanding how language users communicate effectively and strategically in organizational contexts. We suggest that knowing more about what happens in interactions conducted in International Business English and Business English as a Lingua Franca has made an important contribution to English for Specific Purposes research focusing on English for business over the past decade. We will go on to illustrate this below, discussing a number of cases where a Language for Specific Purposes and/or an English for Specific Purposes approach has been used in the investigation of International Business English or Business English as a Lingua Franca.

The lines of research that will be central to this chapter are 1) survey and corpus-based enquiries focusing on International Business English or Business English as a Lingua Franca that have been geared specifically to identifying learner needs for Business English as input for subsequent curriculum and materials design, 2) studies that have offered insights into the characteristics and use of International Business English or Business English as a Lingua

Franca, and 3) contextualized investigations of the pragmatic, intercultural, and language policy issues that play a role in international contexts where International Business English and/or Business English as a Lingua Franca are used. Throughout our discussion, we outline the pedagogical implications the studies profiled have had for English for Specific Purposes. First, however, we briefly discuss the notions of International Business English and Business English as a Lingua Franca and the distinction between them.

Defining Business English as a Lingua Franca and International Business English

Lingua franca communication is communication that takes place between two or more speakers, none of whom speaks that language as their first language. In business, for instance, we talk about the use of Business English as a Lingua Franca when a Chinese business person and a Japanese business person use English to communicate with each other rather than using either Chinese or Japanese. Many researchers have shown that Business English dominates as a lingua franca in many areas of the world, such as Europe and Asia, and it is now generally accepted that Business English as a Lingua Franca is 'neutral' and no longer associated with any of the nations that speak it as a first language. The British scholar David Graddol believes that professional people now require a battery of skills, including a knowledge of English, in order to function in a business context (Graddol, 2006). We will return to this important point later.

International Business English refers to interactions that take place between speakers that do not speak English as their first language and others that do. It is important to make this distinction, particularly in relation to teaching Business English, because the presence of native English speakers in multi-lingual interactions can potentially cause more difficulties for participants. The Finnish researchers Mirjaliisa Charles and Rebecca Marschan-Piekkari, for instance, found evidence of this when they investigated the communication that took place between people at the same organizational level in the multi-national corporation Kone Elevators (Charles & Marschan-Piekkari, 2002, see also Chapter 1). Native speakers of English used a wider range of vocabulary and colloquial expressions, making it difficult for the non-native speakers around them. In contrast, Business English as a Lingua Franca interactions may sometimes be more successful because more limited lexical sets are used by participants. Charles and Marschan-Piekkari suggest that all business people can benefit from training in how to communicate successfully in International Business English and Business English as a Lingua Franca; that non-native speakers can work on extending their Business English skills; and that native speakers can learn how to adjust their Business English to make it more comprehensible for everyone through a process called *accommodation* or *simplification* (see Personal Reflection 2.1).

Personal Reflection 2.1

Think about your experience of using English for professional purposes. Think of a situation where you were communicating in English with a speaker with a first language that was different to yours.

Was there anything that surprised you about the communication?

Did you or the other person use any accommodation strategies, that is, communication strategies designed to make yourselves easier to understand?

Do you find speakers of some first languages easier to understand in English than others?

What is it exactly that makes some non-native speakers of English easier (or harder) to understand than others?

Teaching English as a business lingua franca or international business language

Nickerson (2015), in a discussion of ways to improve the teaching of English for Specific Business Purposes in the Middle East and Asia Pacific regions in particular, suggests that knowing more about "the relationship between communication skills and professional effectiveness, and understanding what determines that relationship, is a crucial element in what we decide to teach" (p. 3). In the rest of this chapter we discuss a number of studies on communication in business contexts by researchers who are also involved in teaching Business English that usefully bridge the gap between international business practices and the Business English classroom. In each case, they either provide input for teaching Business English or they suggest practical applications for use in the Business English classroom that are relevant, up to date, and cognizant of learners' workplace needs.

We start by discussing the multi-method, needs analysis-based project 'Teaching English to meet the needs of business education in Hong Kong' (Bhatia & Candlin, 2001) that was designed specifically to generate recommendations for post-vocational and tertiary Business English teaching in Hong Kong in the late 1990s. The project was conducted in the context of the rapidly changing linguistic landscape in Hong Kong after the British handover to China at the end of the last century. It involved a large number of researchers and tertiary institutions and drew on the views of informants representing a broad range of specialist perspectives, including business students, business professors, Business English practitioners, and business people. More specifically, the Hong Kong project sought to describe the English language demands placed on business students by their subject teachers, by the nature and complexity of the subject discipline(s) they studied, and by the type of academic tasks they were expected to complete as part of their business education. It also aimed to evaluate the effectiveness of the English courses taught at that time in meeting students' English language demands and to offer recommendations to optimize the relevance and scope of Business English teaching in order to better meet students' needs.

Between 1998 and 2000, the researchers collected data using methodologies such as questionnaires (for business students and English department staff) and focus group interviews (with students and business professors). Both business professors and Business English practitioners provided current teaching materials, and writing samples were collected from students. Here, we will focus on two investigations from project researchers that highlight two informant perspectives: a survey of business professors which was based on teachers' viewpoints, and a needs analysis survey of banking professionals which reflects the professionals' perspective (Chew, 2005; Jackson, 2005).

Business professors at five tertiary institutions in Hong Kong were interviewed to determine business students' cross-disciplinary English language needs. The topics that were covered included the status of students' English, the specific English language demands of the various business sub-disciplines, and students' progress through their programme. The professors interviewed represented a range of specializations that business students are likely to encounter in their studies, such as marketing, management, international business, accountancy, and law.

Although there was a lot of variety in the professors' viewpoints, they generally agreed that for many students, disciplinary variation within the specializations in undergraduate degree programmes was the most difficult aspect of their studies. The professors signalled a clear need for a dedicated course for first-year students that could equip them with the English language skills they lacked for use in business contexts, followed by discipline-specific English for Specific Purposes courses in the later years of their programme when they specialized in one or more of the business sub-disciplines. The study showed that the situations in which appropriate Business English teaching materials need to be developed are often complex, in the Hong Kong case not only because Cantonese was used next to English at all times, but also because students were expected to cope with a wide range of sub-disciplines during their studies, each with its own discipline-specific communication tasks, genres, and discourse.

The second study from the Hong Kong project reveals the complexity of the situation faced by Business English curriculum developers in Hong Kong in relation to the English-language needs of new entrants in the Hong Kong banking sector. Through interviews with new bank employees at four Hong Kong banks and a follow-up survey, it was possible to identify the communicative tasks and associated English language skills that were required of these employees in the workplace on a daily basis. The survey and interviews explored issues such as time spent communicating in English every day, the communicative tasks engaged in, which English language skills were used most, and the difficulties that bank employees encountered when using English. The study revealed a professional context in which most written tasks were conducted in English while the majority of spoken tasks were carried out in Cantonese. Most of the people interviewed reported difficulties with the English language demands posed by communicative tasks in the workplace, and, as we have suggested is often the case in multilingual organizations, they also highlighted the difficulties of communicating with colleagues whose first language was English.

In Chapter 8 of this volume we will include a discussion of a study by Evans (2012) which investigated the use of English in business email. Evans' study also looked at Business English as a Lingua Franca in Hong Kong and provides concrete suggestions as to how authentic email tasks can be created for the Business English classroom.

Task 2.1 asks you to consider how you might assess the Business English needs of your students (or your future students).

Task 2.1 Assessing learner needs

Design a project in which you prepare to assess the needs of the learners that you deal with (or that you will be dealing with in the future).

Are your learners more likely to be using Business English as a Lingua Franca or International Business English?

Who will they be interacting with?

What consequences would this have for the language and tasks that you will need to focus on?

Decide what information you would need to collect in order to determine their needs both now and in the future, and then think of different ways in which you could collect that information.

Analyzing Business English as a Lingua Franca

In this section, we briefly discuss two recent studies aimed specifically at determining the nature and characteristics of Business English as a Lingua Franca (Kankaanranta & Planken, 2010; Kankaanranta & Louhiala-Salminen, 2010). What makes these studies interesting – and rare – is their approach, in that they privilege the perspectives of business professionals operating internationally, using self-reports on how they themselves view and experience Business English as a Lingua Franca and how they see it contributing (or not) to their individual success at work. The studies were part of the large-scale project 'Does business know how: the role of communication in business know-how of globalized operations' run by researchers at the department of International Business Communication at Aalto University, Finland (formerly the Helsinki School of Economics) and involving multiple sub-projects and researchers from various countries. The two accounts discussed here report on the sub-project that focused on the notion of 'BELF competence' (Business English as a Lingua Franca competence), which the researchers regard as an integral and essential part of the communication know-how and business expertise expected of business professionals operating in a globalized context today. The sub-project aimed to increase understanding of the various dimensions of Business English competence through business professionals' own perspectives on using it, and in doing so to explore their Business English as a Lingua Franca experience. The researchers reported the findings from a large-scale online survey of around 1,000 business professionals in five globally operating companies based in Finland (Kankaanranta & Louhiala-Salminen, 2010), and follow-up in-depth interviews with globally operating business professionals from Finland and the Netherlands (Kankaanranta & Planken, 2010).

The project's outcomes, as reported in these two accounts, show that Business English as a Lingua Franca can be characterized as a "simplified, hybridized, and highly dynamic communication code", and that competence in using it "calls for clarity and accuracy of content (rather than linguistic correctness), and knowledge of business-specific vocabulary and genre conventions (rather than only 'general' English)" (Kankaanranta & Planken, 2010, p. 380). Informants' understanding of 'competence' and 'proficiency' in Business English as a Lingua Franca is largely pragmatic and usually overlaps with their ideas about business communication competence, business competence, and business know-how more generally.

Because Business English as a Lingua Franca encounters can involve non-native speakers from a variety of cultures, the relational orientation in particular – that is, maintaining a good relationship and managing rapport – is perceived by Business English as a Lingua Franca users as an integral aspect of competence. Business English as a Lingua Franca competence as a whole is seen as an essential component of the business knowledge required in today's global business environment, although at the same time it seems that to be successful in their work, "globally operating professionals need at least two languages to do their work, not only English but also their mother tongue" (Kankaanranta & Planken, 2010, p. 398).

The project outcomes are relevant for Business English teaching in a number of ways. First, they indicate that in real life contexts, business competence (operational know-how), a knowledge of how people communicate in business contexts and genre rules are considered more important, and more useful 'on the job', than grammatical and idiomatic correctness. Consequently, it would seem that in international contexts of work, native-like fluency is not a criterion that determines success. In fact, it might not even be required, given that the project showed that most interactions in international business take place, in Business English as a Lingua Franca, between non-native speakers of English. This suggests that a shift in the criteria and foci applied in Business English teaching is also in order. Indeed as we discussed earlier, as long ago as 2002,

Charles and Marschan-Piekkari suggested that it would be better for internationally operating corporations to train their native English-speaking employees to accommodate their language to their non-native English-speaking business counterparts instead of teaching non-native English-speaking employees to achieve mastery in English (Charles & Marschan-Piekkari, 2002, see also Task 2.2 below). Second, given the way business knowledge and know-how appear to be intertwined with Business English as a Lingua Franca, Louhiala-Salminen and Kankaanranta (2011) recommend that teachers and trainers should integrate as much business knowledge and awareness of the business context into Business English courses as possible (see also Zhang, 2007). Third, they suggest that strategies that work well in promoting communication effectiveness for business communication in general work just as well in Business English as a Lingua Franca. They base this on the observation that interviewees' perceptions about successful BELF use, and the success factors they named were surprisingly similar to those found in communication textbooks. This suggests that such textbook strategies can be used as guidelines in teaching Business English to business people who will be using it as a lingua franca, and that they can serve as criteria for assessing Business English competence. At the same time, as the appropriateness of specific communication strategies is context-bound, Louhiala-Salminen and Kankaanranta (2011) observe that "students need to be trained to be flexibly competent", in that the "ultimate aim [...] should be to do a particular job required in the particular assignment" (p. 258). And ultimately, of course, for students this aim extends beyond the Business English classroom to the real world that is the international workplace in which they will end up working.

Task 2.2 Using English as an international business language

Charles and Marschan-Piekkari (2002) suggest that it would be better to train native speakers of Business English to accommodate their non-native colleagues, rather than the other way around. Think of three ways in which you could do this in a classroom setting.

What would you include in a course designed to improve the use of Business English when it is being used as an international business language?

Business English as a Lingua Franca and International Business English in context

In the past two decades, Business English as a Lingua Franca and International Business English have increasingly been studied by researchers who want to gain an understanding of the characteristics of language used for business (or business discourse) more generally – an acknowledgement that the majority of interactions in international business nowadays do not involve native speakers of English. A number of such studies have taken a contextualized approach: they have looked at how the business context – as it is reflected in sociopragmatic, cultural, and language policy issues – plays a role in interactions between business professionals using English as a lingua franca. For example in their 2005 study, Louhiala-Salminen et al. studied the impact of introducing Business English as a Lingua Franca as a corporate language following two Nordic mergers. We discuss two other related studies on multiparty, intercultural meetings in English, by Poncini (2004) and Rogerson-Revell (2007), in Chapter 4 of this volume. Both these studies considered the nature of International Business English and in particular how it is shaped by corporate and national cultures. Rogerson-Revell also explored how the use of English as a common language impacts on the professional effectiveness of non-native users.

Louhiala-Salminen et al. (2005) have characterized Business English as a Lingua Franca as a "'neutral' and shared communication code": neutral because "none of the speakers can claim it as his/her mother tongue", and shared as "it is used for conducting business within the global discourse community, whose members are Business English as a Lingua Franca users and communicators in their own right – not 'non-native speakers' or 'learners'" (Louhiala-Salminen et al., 2005, pp. 403–4). In their study, they investigated the consequences of introducing English as the official language for Finnish and Swedish employees after two international mergers, each between a Finnish and a Swedish company. Using a survey and interviews, they focused on the two groups' perceptions of each other's communication and cultures, against the backdrop of the Business English as a Lingua Franca interactions they produced when working together in the newly merged companies. The Swedish and Finnish were asked, for instance, about their language choice in different situations, and about the characteristics they considered to be 'typical' of Swedish or Finnish styles of communication. From transcripts of videoed meetings between the two nationalities, researchers used corpus analysis to establish the extent to which the characteristics identified as 'typical' of each other's communication were reflected in the discourse produced by members of each culture. The researchers hypothesized that although Business English as a Lingua Franca can be seen as a neutral communication code, in that every user starts out on an equal footing as a non-native speaker, this does not mean that the resulting language produced is also culture-neutral. They expected Business English as a Lingua Franca speakers to bring "their own culture-bound views of how encounters should be conducted" to interactions, as well as "discourse practices" inspired by their first languages (Louhiala-Salminen et al., 2005, p. 404).

The study showed that employees' lingua franca use increased after the mergers, with employees of both nationalities, at all levels and in all business units using English for practically all internal communication, including telephone calls and meetings. Their language choice was pragmatic, depending on the target group and their partner's language skills (some Finnish employees in the company where Swedish had been the official language before the merger continued to speak Swedish with Swedish colleagues), the status of English as the new corporate language, and the medium and genre of communication (for example, spoken versus written, meetings versus chats at the coffee machine). Employees reported difficulties with foreign languages – including Business English as a Lingua Franca for both nationalities, and Swedish for the Finnish – in providing nuances in discussions, small talk, and when giving an opinion in meetings (compare this with the findings from Rogerson-Revell's study discussed in Chapter 4). Overall, the most problematic area signalled by both nationalities and in both companies was the use of foreign languages – including Business English as a Lingua Franca – in spoken rather than written communication.

The study also confirmed the authors' assumption that the production of Business English as a Lingua Franca reflects participants' cultural backgrounds, and that they continue to regard other speakers from the perspective of their own national framework. With respect to typical Finnish or Swedish business communication, Swedes were regarded as "discussive" and "wordy", while Finns were seen as "direct" and "economical with words" (Louhiala-Salminen et al., 2005, p. 408). The participants in the study talked about their own communication and their counterparts' communication in the same kind of way, although they had different ways of describing what they considered effective communication. The Finns, for example, saw themselves as good communicators because they were "factual" and "direct", while the Swedes described similar traits in the Finns as "blunt". The Swedes described themselves positively as "discussive" and "democratic", while the Finns saw the Swedes as "wordy" above anything else (Louhiala-Salminen et al., 2005, p. 409). The researchers' assumption that users transfer first language patterns to Business English as a Lingua Franca was also confirmed. In meetings between the two nationalities, the Swedes' Business English as a Lingua Franca reflected an interpersonal orientation, with queries, questions, hedging, and other forms of meta-discourse intended to orient the hearer to the discourse. In contrast, the Finns' Business English as a Lingua Franca was more task-focused, reflecting a lower level of interpersonal orientation.

The study is insightful because it describes real-life Business English as a Lingua Franca, provides evidence of the factors that affect its use, and improves our understanding of the impact of opting for English as a common corporate language, even in countries where English proficiency is considered to be high. The study also pinpoints an important characteristic of Business English as a Lingua Franca: the differences noted in the communication styles of Swedish versus Finnish Business English as a Lingua Franca provide evidence that Business English as a Lingua Franca is not culture-neutral, but rather "a conduit of its speaker's communication culture" (Louhiala-Salminen et al., 2005, p. 417). This finding has a number of obvious implications for Business English pedagogy. Firstly, the notion of Business English as a Lingua Franca as a shared, 'functional' code needs to be offset against the fact that in Business English as a Lingua Franca, users rely on their own, not necessarily shared, first language patterns, culture(s), and culturally determined practices. What this implies for Business English teaching and materials development is that native-speaker or near-native speaker norms for English (i.e. levels of competence in grammar, pronunciation, etc.) may not be directly relevant for setting course objectives or for determining course focus – that is, which aspects of language deserve attention, or which materials are most suitable. Ideally, course objectives should relate specifically to Business English as a Lingua Franca users and should follow from a consideration of a number of different Business English as a Lingua Franca characteristics, the communication tasks and settings in which it is used, and the specific difficulties, needs, and motivations associated with its use. The authors suggest that when teaching learners to use Business English for international business, the 'BELF perspective' should always be kept in mind. Users should be trained "to see themselves as communicators who have real jobs to do and needs to fulfil", and it is therefore "these jobs and needs that should be emphasized [in courses], not the language they use to carry them out" (Louhiala-Salminen et al., 2005, pp. 418–19). Later in this volume, we will discuss the implications of these research findings for the development of appropriate teaching materials.

The authors also recommend that because of the variation in cultural frameworks that Business English as a Lingua Franca users can bring to intercultural encounters, users should be sensitized to interpreting and using "contextual clues" and be trained to recognize the "situational presuppositions of their counterparts in an interaction" (Louhiala-Salminen et al., 2005, p. 419). Training people's listening skills is seen as important in this respect, because it is only through listening to what Business English as a Lingua Franca users "say and imply" that such learning objectives can be attained (p. 419). Finally, the authors recommend that learners should be made aware of their own and others' cultural communication patterns and relevant discourse practices and conventions, so that they can learn to become more flexible users of Business English as a Lingua Franca.

Summary

In this chapter, we have looked at Business English as a Lingua Franca and International Business English and the ways in which they have been investigated over the past decade. We have discussed the contextual and discursive turn that Business English has taken as a result, and we have looked at the shift away from native-speaker models towards the accommodation of different ways of using Business English as a Lingua Franca in multilingual business interactions. In the next chapter, we will look at spoken business English in general, and how this has been incorporated into Business English teaching materials.

Part II

Spoken Business English

Chapter 3

Introducing Spoken Business English

Introduction

In Part II, we consider how spoken Business English has been studied by researchers taking an English for Specific Business Purposes approach. On the basis of a number of selected studies, this chapter looks at some of the main methods that have been used to study aspects of meetings, negotiations, and service encounters in English, and how business talk in such contexts is used to achieve work-related and relational goals. We also consider how the discourse-based focus in research on spoken Business English has shown how the context in which interactions take place influences both the Business English and the discursive and interactional strategies used by participants. Finally, we consider ways in which this type of study can inform the teaching of Business English. Chapter 4 continues the discussion of spoken Business English by considering intercultural business encounters, while Chapter 5 considers how recent research taking an English for Specific Business Purposes approach has been incorporated into teaching and training focusing on spoken Business English.

A good deal of the time, doing business requires professionals to engage in business talk – i.e. to use spoken Business English in a variety of workplace settings. Business people spend much of their time in planned meetings, discussing strategy or sales deals, dividing tasks, or assessing the progress of projects, for example. Formal meetings tend to involve multiple parties (more than two people) and are usually led by a chairperson who makes sure that the interaction proceeds in an orderly way and participants get the chance to contribute to the discussion more or less equally. Typically, a meeting will follow the points set out in a written agenda which is circulated to participants beforehand. As a result – and provided the chairperson is effective – formal, planned meetings proceed in a structured and predictable way. At the same time, many meetings that take place in the workplace are informal. They come about spontaneously and may therefore be more loosely structured (Koester, 2006). Interestingly, then, for a meeting to be recognized as such by participants, not all of the 'rules' associated with this type of business interaction need to be followed. For instance, although spontaneous work-related encounters between colleagues may not have a regulating chairperson or a written agenda and are unlikely to ever generate written minutes, we still regard them intuitively as meetings.

Negotiation is another important form of spoken communication in the workplace. Negotiating occurs in situations where at least two parties or participants have shared but also differing interests with regard to a particular issue or topic. They therefore talk with each other in order to reach an agreement that is mutually satisfactory for everyone involved. Negotiations can be about a variety of topics, such as the deadline for a marketing project (with colleagues), a salary increase (with a boss), or the pricing of a particular product line (with a customer or client). The goal of negotiating can be to reach an understanding, to resolve a problem or difference in opinion, or to gain an advantage in a particular sales deal.

A third form of spoken communication in business is the service encounter, which can be defined broadly as a business interaction, often over the telephone, in which the provision of information is central (Koester, 2006). For instance, a customer may call a service employee to book a flight or hotel room, or to ask a question regarding the guarantee for a particular product. Nowadays many such service encounters are outsourced to call centres and dealt with by call service agents (see also Lockwood's (2012) study in Chapter 1). As service employees and call centre agents often work to a script when responding to customer requests and questions, service encounters, like meetings and negotiations, have a standardized and predictable format. We will discuss these three types of business interaction in more detail below.

Characteristics of spoken Business English

In her publication *The Language of Work*, Koester (2004) refers to a corpus of real-life language data from a variety of workplaces in the US and UK in order to illustrate how Business English is used in different written and spoken forms of business communication including meetings, negotiations, and service encounters. She also outlines what it is that sets this 'business talk' apart from everyday conversation, drawing on the notion of "institutional talk" as defined by Drew and Heritage (1992).

First, according to Koester, business talk takes place in organizational contexts and involves participants in a variety of different roles and relationships. For instance, while one business interaction may involve a group of co-workers in a team meeting, another may be between a manager and a subordinate engaged in a performance appraisal interview, or between an employee and a customer in a shop. As a result, business interactions are likely to be unequal or asymmetrical, in the sense that one participant may have more power (e.g. manager versus trainee) or knowledge (e.g. service employee versus customer) than another. This asymmetry will be reflected in what participants are allowed to say or contribute in a particular interaction, and in the language that they use to do so. As we will see later, taking into account contextual factors such as the institutional roles that people have, the social distance between them (i.e. how well they know each other), and the power difference between them in a work relationship has been an essential part of the study of Business English in different settings. This is because these factors affect and shape the language and the interactional and discursive strategies that speakers and writers use.

Second, Koester notes that business talk is primarily topic-centred and task-oriented, because it is geared to helping participants to do their work, to solve specific work-related problems or take work-related decisions, and ultimately, to fulfil the organization's goals. Third, the structure of business interactions – at least formal ones – is to a large extent standardized, in that a particular spoken form (e.g. a sales negotiation) tends to progress through a number of set stages and involves specific turn-taking rules; that is, rules regarding who speaks at what point in an interaction. For example, the chairperson usually opens and closes a meeting, and summarizes the ongoing discussion at different intervals.

Finally, business talk is different from everyday conversation because it involves specific, professional lexis (i.e. business vocabulary and technical jargon) relevant to the participants' specialism (e.g. financial control or logistics), the business discipline (e.g. marketing or human resource management), and the company's core activity (e.g. manufacturing or service industry). In 2000, Nelson investigated the differences between authentic Business English and authentic everyday English using his Business English Corpus (BEC) for British and US native-speaker business talk, and the British National Corpus (BNC) for everyday English. He found that the words and phrases in the BEC represented a limited number of semantic categories (e.g. people in business, business activities, places of business) and combinations of words, compared with those in the BNC. The BEC lexis largely related to business people, companies, institutions, money, business events, places of business, time, modes of communication, and technology, and was more positive in nature (using words such as *growth, realize, achieve, successful, improve*) than the lexis in the BNC. In addition, most adjectives in the BEC referred to things such as products and companies rather than people, and emphasized action and dynamism (using words such as *systematic, sustainable, applicable, functional*), rather than emotion. Nelson's findings (see also Nelson, 2006) suggest that specific areas of lexis are central to authentic Business English and distinct from everyday English. (For a discussion of the study and its applications in teaching Business English, see Bargiela-Chiappini et al., 2013.)

Koester notes that the distinctions between business talk and everyday talk are equally applicable to business writing versus general writing (Koester, 2004, p. 2). As we discuss a selection of studies on spoken Business English in what follows, we will see that each study has helped to throw light on one or more of the specific characteristics of business talk outlined above.

In Task 3.1, you are asked to consider some of the characteristics of business talk in light of a negotiation situation you were recently involved in.

Task 3.1 Negotiation

For this task, we would like you to recall a recent instance in which you negotiated with someone at work, at university, or in a shop. Describe the encounter, using the questions below to guide you:

Goal: What was the goal of the negotiation?

Power/knowledge: Was the relationship between you and the other[s] equal or asymmetrical? How did this affect what you contributed and the language you used?

Structure: Was the encounter structured? How? To what extent was the structure of the interaction predictable?

Lexis: Did you use any context-specific or topic-specific vocabulary? What words did you use that were specific?

How did the interaction differ from an everyday conversation?

Would you say it qualifies as business talk in the way Koester (2004) describes it?

The importance of research based on real language data

In Chapter 1, we referred to an early study of Business English by Williams (1988). This study highlighted the fact that the language presented in teaching materials on business meetings at the time was not necessarily a true reflection of the language used in real-life business meetings. Williams found that the examples of Business English in textbooks were different to, and less complex than, the Business English used in actual meetings. We have noted that this mismatch between language in materials and actual language in the workplace continues to exist in many Business English textbooks (see St John, 1996; Nickerson, 2005). We aim to show in Parts II and III that what makes the research we refer to particularly useful for the teaching of Business English is that it is based on analyses of authentic language; that is, real-life Business English generated by professionals in a variety of workplace contexts, to realize various forms of business communication or business genres. As we have seen, the concept of genre (i.e. the type of business text or business encounter, see also Chapter 1) has been important in studies aiming to account for variation in Business English across different communication contexts. (See Chapter 6 for a discussion of genre in relation to written Business English.) Genre-based studies (i.e. studies of business letters or meetings, for example) have provided valuable insights into the functional, linguistic, and structural characteristics of different forms of Business English at work. Particularly with regard to written Business English, this has also greatly influenced how Business English writing is taught (see Part III). In addition, because most genre-based studies have tended to be strongly data-driven (in that they use a collection or corpus of business texts or interactions for the analysis), genre-based research has generated many authentic examples of Business English. We will see that authentic examples of Business English can – and increasingly do – form the basis for more realistic teaching materials, and for classroom tasks for Business English curricula that reflect real-life business interactions.

Recent studies of workplace language have begun to employ corpus linguistic techniques (i.e. methods allowing systematic examination of frequently occurring lexis and recurring lexico-grammatical patterns in authentic texts or interactions) to investigate linguistic variation in and across business genres, in order to identify the linguistic forms that are used with specific communication functions (Flowerdew, 2011). Such quantitative approaches also provide a potentially productive framework for the study of Business English, as demonstrated in a number of projects including the work of Almut Koester on spoken (and written) Business English in the American and British Office Talk (ABOT) corpus (Koester, 2006; 2012), Handford's (2010) study of business meetings in the Cambridge and Nottingham Business English Corpus (CANBEC) corpus, and the work of Holmes and colleagues on spoken Business English data collected in New Zealand workplaces as part of the long-running Language in the Workplace Project (Holmes, 2000) which we introduced briefly in Chapter 1. These are all data-driven studies of (mostly) spoken Business English, whose findings can be used as input for authentic, relevant Business English teaching materials that can raise students' awareness of the difference between Business English and everyday English, the Business English used in various spoken genres, and the way in which contextual factors influence business discourse (see for example Brown & Lewis, 2002; Koester, 2004). All three projects are discussed below and elsewhere in this volume.

Discourse-based studies of spoken Business English

Research on spoken business genres has tended to look at formalized and established interaction types which progress through a set series of stages and are characterized by a clear beginning, middle, and end. Because of their regularities, these specific interaction types, such as meetings, negotiations, and service encounters, are more suitable for formal analysis (see Koester, 2006). Although we intuitively regard meetings and negotiations as separate types of business encounter, meetings may at times also feature negotiating. As both types of encounter are used for problem-solving, negotiation (like decision-making) may occur within meetings in situations where participants have diverging opinions or interests but need to reach agreement (i.e. need to solve the 'problem'). In other words, meeting and negotiating may at times be intertwined.

We consider the ways in which different text and interaction types are networked and integrated in more detail when we look at intertextuality and interdiscursivity in Chapter 9.

Language-based studies of spoken Business English have been important to teaching in that they have identified and described various types of business encounters (e.g. meetings and negotiations) and shown us the factors that influence and shape the discourse used in them. Studies on meetings and negotiations are well represented in the literature on workplace talk. Boden (1994), for example, studied talk in a variety of organizations in the US. Although she looked at naturally occurring business talk in various contexts, both formal and informal, her specific focus was on talk in meetings. Using ethnomethodology (i.e. analyzing practitioners' accounts of the methods they use and their experiences at work) and Conversation Analysis (which looks, for example, at the way in which turn-taking and topic switches signal social order in conversations), Boden showed how talk in meetings brings about action, and how that talk is influenced by the social context; that is, by the business culture and the shared practices in the organization. At the same time, she demonstrated how the relationship between talk and the context in which it is used is a reciprocal one. While the context influences the business talk, that business talk, in turn, shapes and constitutes (i.e. creates) the organizational context. Boden argues convincingly that meetings are therefore central to management and managing, and specifically to organizing structure and accomplishing action. According to Boden, people in organizations essentially "talk" their organizations into being (p. 16).

Since Boden's seminal publication, many discourse-based studies of business talk have continued to investigate how the context in which encounters take place shapes (and to a certain extent determines) participants' discursive and interactional strategies – i.e. the Business English they use. Bargiela-Chiappini and Harris (1997), for example, carried out a comparative analysis of Italian and British corporate meetings in order to examine how participants create coherence in interactions through their use of lexis, personal pronouns, metaphoric language, and discourse markers. Their detailed analysis shows how meetings progress on the basis of shared themes, and that the development of these themes is achieved jointly and interactionally by the participants in a meeting. Furthermore, regardless of whether the meetings were being held in Italian or English, they followed a common three-phase structure of 1) opening, 2) debating, and 3) closing. There were also differences between the two sets of meetings – for example with respect to the extent to which participants and chairpersons contributed in the different phases. Another difference was that the Italians used metaphoric language to realize coherence to a far greater extent than the British. What this work highlights is that the discourse and interactional structure of business meetings is influenced not only by institutional factors such as the business culture in which a meeting takes place – i.e. by organizational practices – but also by the cultural backgrounds of the meeting participants – i.e. the different cultural communication practices (and languages) participants bring into, and therefore incorporate into, the discourse of intercultural encounters (Bargiela-Chiappini & Harris, 1997). In Part III, we will see that similar insights into the way contextual factors influence and shape Business English have been generated by genre-based studies on written forms of workplace communication such as emails and letters.

As part of the Language in the Workplace Project, Holmes and Stubbe's 2003 publication presents the findings of their analyses of discourse in both formal and informal meetings in New Zealand companies (80 meetings at nine different organizations). The main focus in their project was on the way people maintain and signal their working relationships with others in terms of power and politeness. Holmes and Stubbe found that the meetings in their corpus commonly progressed through three main phases: 1) an opening section, 2) a central development section in which the points on the agenda are discussed, and 3) a closing section. This suggests a typical structure for meetings, or in genre terms, a generic set of "moves" (Swales 1990) that participants intui- tively recognize and that helps them identify the interaction (i.e. the meeting) as that specific type or genre. Bargiela-Chiappini and Harris (1997) also iden- tified these three stages in both the Italian and British business meetings they analyzed, which suggests that this sequence of moves characterizes the genre across cultures.

At the level of discourse, Holmes and Stubbe's study highlights many of the strategies participants use in meetings to manage interaction; that is, to regulate and guarantee orderly progress through the meeting event. For instance, the parti- cipants used strategies such as summarizing the discussion, reaching and ratifying agreement, asking for clarification or explanation, and keeping to the agenda. In contrast, chairpersons used strategies such as assigning turns to speak, moving to the next point on the agenda, or opening and closing particular (sub) phases of the meeting. Discourse strategies were also employed by the partici- pants to explicitly exercise power (i.e. to influence the progress of a meeting or the decision-making process) and to manage relationships (by emphasizing or reducing social distance between themselves and others in a meeting). For example, managers would use more polite – i.e. indirect – linguistic strategies in interactions if they wanted to achieve conversational goals in a cooperative manner and maintain their authority, regardless of whether the other person was a fellow manager or a worker lower down the hierarchy. In contrast, workers used different politeness strategies with their peers than with managers. Again, this shows how contextual factors – in this case the power distance between participants – influence the discourse.

Holmes and Stubbe (2003) also showed how meeting practices (i.e. the agreed ways of doing things among participants) influence meeting discourse. For example, meetings often included episodes of small talk and humour, or 'social talk'. Participants would use this social talk to break the ice, diffuse a tense situation or disagreement, relieve boredom, or allow a short break from work-related discussions. Holmes and Stubbe describe such social discourse strategies as a tool to manage work relationships. Social talk allows participants to express solidarity and to reinforce group feeling and workplace harmony. They note that it essentially "functions like knitting; it can be easily taken up and just as easily dropped" (p. 106). This points to another important feature of business talk; namely that it is primarily, but not exclusively, task-oriented and work-related. As Holmes and Stubbe's findings show, relational work is also achieved in meetings through discourse and alternates with transactional talk; that is, talk about work and not about the relationship between the people involved. We will return to a discussion of the importance of discursive and linguistic strategies that signal the relational dimension in spoken business communication in later chapters when we specifically look at rapport management in intercultural business meetings.

In comparison to the wealth of negotiation research in other disciplines such as business and management studies, there have been relatively few studies that have considered negotiation at the level of language; that is, as a type of spoken business discourse. Yet like meetings, negotiations have featured prominently in the literature on workplace and business discourse over the past decades. Two volumes published in the 1990s, one edited by Ehlich and Wagner (1995) and the other by Firth (1995), bring together a selection of early discourse-based negotiation studies. Although not all of the studies in these volumes feature negotiations in Business English, they offer insights on the structural elements of the genre of negotiation, the strategies negotiators use to achieve conversational goals, and the factors that influence the discourse. Such insights are essential for creating teaching materials that reflect authentic practices and authentic examples of negotiation episodes and the discourse strategies used within them.

Charles, in an early language-oriented study dating from 1996, investigated the discourse of negotiations based on a corpus of six British business negotiations (ca. 15 hours of spoken Business English). She aimed to demonstrate the interdependence between the discourse in the negotiations and the context within which that discourse was produced (Charles, 1996). The contextual factors she was interested in were the nature of the business relationship (established or new) and the roles of the participants (buyer or seller). Charles looked at the structural organization of the negotiations, and at the discourse in terms of politeness (relational) strategies and tactical (transactional) strategies. She compared the 'buyer and seller talk' within and across two sets of negotiations, one consisting of new relationship negotiations (whose participants had not done business before) and the other consisting of old relationship negotiations (whose participants had an established business relationship). She also conducted interviews with the participants to gain information about their business relationship and experiences.

Charles identified a three-part structure in the negotiations, consisting of 1) initiation (beginning stages to establish positions), 2) development (discussion of points on the agenda and bargaining phase), and 3) ending (the 'warming down' of the interaction). Also, for each of the participant types (buyers and sellers), she distinguished a number of prototypical tactics (or discourse strategies) that reflected their respective roles in the negotiations. According to Charles, these are in fact the tactics – or verbal behaviour – that we expect negotiators to use in their "status-bound" position of buyer or seller (Charles, 1996, p. 23). Buyers displayed four strategies: 1) express a certain degree of disinterest in the sellers' products, 2) point out shortcomings of the product or give other reasons why not to buy from the seller, 3) emphasize the high standard required from the seller, and 4) exert some control over the seller and the situation (Charles, 1996, p. 23). Sellers, on the other hand, used four tactics: 1) show enthusiasm for the product, but also interest in the buyer and the deal, 2) draw attention to appealing characteristics of the product, 3) emphasize their trustworthiness, their likability as a business partner and the high standards they adhere to, and 4) show that they accept that the buyer has control over the situation, but also that control is shared (Charles, 1996, p. 23). The negotiators in the study used these different sets of tactical strategies consistently, which Charles took as evidence that roles (i.e. buyer versus seller) do influence negotiation discourse. The buyers and sellers also differed with respect to the way they managed the interaction: they introduced different types of topics and used different rhetorical (i.e. persuasive) moves.

In contrast, the sellers as well as the buyers made similar use of linguistic politeness strategies, particularly a form of politeness known as *hedging*. In general, *hedges* are used to soften or mitigate so-called face-threatening utterances such as refusals, rejections of offers, counter-offers, and other moves that are threatening to the hearer because they signal disagreement or non-compliance (see Brown & Levinson, 1987). In a negotiation context, for example, explanations or justifications for rejecting an offer (e.g. *"I really don't have much room to move in my position,* so I can't accept that offer") constitute hedges, as do indirect, vague formulations of face-threatening moves (e.g. *"Well, let's see, maybe* you could do *something a little more"* rather than "Make me a better offer"). Interestingly, the buyers and sellers in Charles' study also used hedges where they would not normally be expected – in combination with positive, face-supporting moves (such as praise for the seller's product or enthusiasm for the buyer's flexibility, etc.) which, theoretically, do not require a strategy such as hedging to minimize the threat to face (see Brown & Levinson, 1987). Charles suggests that this seemingly inappropriate use of hedges signals what she terms "professional face" (1996, p. 24). This is the negotiator's need to maintain a suitable degree of professional distance and reserve in the business relationship, which amounts to yet another status-bound expectation.

Finally, Charles noted a clear shift from the status-bound (expected) verbal behaviour in the new relationship negotiations to more personal and informal discourse, and less rigidly structured interactions, in the old relationship negotiations. This was reflected in a strategy used by sellers in the old relationship negotiations. When they introduced the topic of a problem with the deal (for the seller), they would explicitly indicate in what way the problem (e.g. too low a counter-offer or pressure on delivery times) would affect them negatively at an individual, personal level, and that the problem would not just be detrimental to sales performance or the company. In doing so, they effectively appealed to the buyers – at a personal level – to help them avoid the problem. According to Charles, this type of personalization reflects the absence of professional, status-bound behaviour in the old business relationships, and contributes to the impression that the old relationship negotiations were more friendly.

To end this section, we briefly turn our attention to the genre of telephone service encounters. As mentioned earlier, telephone service encounters are interactions between a service employee or call centre agent and a customer whose purpose is to provide certain customer services, such as taking a product order or dealing with enquiries about products or services. In the latter type of encounter, where giving information is central, service encounters nearly always involve the speech act of request. A speech act involves someone saying something specific that simultaneously performs a particular function or action. In addition to requesting, examples include promising, greeting, ordering, instructing, and closing a meeting. The idea is that by uttering the speech act (e.g. "That brings me to the end of this presentation"), the speaker simultaneously performs the action (e.g. of ending the presentation). As a result, speech acts are also referred to as "performatives" (Austin, 1962). We will see in Chapters 4 and 5 that speech acts have been used as a unit of analysis in research on business talk (see also our earlier discussion of Charles' (1996) study, in which she analyzed politeness in face-threatening speech acts).

In telephone service encounters, the roles of participants are generally clear. Customers have the right to request something, and the service agent has the obligation to help them by fulfilling their requests or answering their questions. These service encounters are essentially aimed at problem-solving: the customer has a certain need – for service, knowledge, or advice – that has to be fulfilled. In addition, they may at some stage involve negotiating about different options (i.e. solutions for the problem) that may be available. Because telephone service encounters are usually based on scripts, they follow a standard format, and the turn-taking structure of different phases in a service call is predictable. Usually, the telephone operator speaks first, greeting the caller. After an optional return greeting, the caller then makes the request. In the next turn, the telephone operator provides the information or asks the caller for further details regarding his or her request.

The opening sequence of telephone service encounters was studied by Economidou-Kogetsidis (2005), who looked at politeness strategies in Greek and British callers' initial requests in service calls to an airline's call centre. She collected a corpus of 200 authentic opening requests: 100 produced in Greek by Greek native speakers and 100 produced in English by English native speakers. She analyzed them with regard to the degree of directness that was used to formulate the speech act of request, distinguishing three levels of directness in her analytical framework (p. 260). In the most direct strategy (Strategy 1), the request is formulated as an imperative or order (e.g. "Tell me what flights you have to Barcelona"). Strategy 2 is less direct and makes use of so-called conventional indirectness. The most conventionalized way of making a request indirect is to formulate it as a question (e.g. "Could you tell me what time the flight to Rome departs?"). In the final and least direct strategy (Strategy 3), the request is formulated as a hint. Hints are formulated in such an unconventional (often ambiguous) way that it takes much more work than Strategies 1 and 2 on the part of the hearer to understand that what the speaker is saying constitutes a request (Economidou-Kogetsidis, 2005, p. 260). Economidou-Kogetsidis found that while the three requesting strategies were used in both Greek and English, there were also clear differences between the two cultures with regard to the frequency with which the strategies were used. For instance, the Greeks used the most direct strategy (Strategy 1) to formulate their requests more often than the English (76% of the Greek versus 42% of the English requests). The requests in English were more often formulated using conventional indirectness (Strategy 2, 46%) or hints (Strategy 3, 16%) than was the case for the Greek requests (11% and 8% respectively). These findings strongly suggest that in the context of telephone service encounters, requests are formulated more directly in Greek than in English.

Overall, the findings from the study demonstrate that different cultures prefer different politeness (i.e. directness) strategies. This may be a result of the fact that they "have differing perceptions of social reality" (Economidou-Kogetsidis, 2005, p. 269). Findings such as these are relevant to teaching Business English in that they can be used to raise students' awareness of cultural variation in the realization of discourse strategies – or in this case of particular speech acts like requesting – and of the potential consequences of such variation in intercultural business encounters. For example, if Greeks had similar degrees of directness in the English they used in exchanges with their British counterparts, how would those counterparts perceive them? The findings are therefore particularly informative in relation to teaching Business English to non-native speakers of English. We discuss such applications in teaching further in the next chapter and in Part V of this volume.

In Task 3.2, you are asked to consider the speech act of requesting and how you would formulate a request in your own language and in a language that is not your first language.

Task 3.2 Request strategies

Imagine a situation in which you call a hotel to enquire about the price of rooms. How would you formulate the task in your first language, and in a language that is not your first language? Make sure you use English (as your own or another language) as part of this assignment!

In terms of the three levels of directness distinguished in the study by Economidou-Kogetsidis, what strategy or strategies did you use to formulate the requests in English and in your own language?

Did you use any politeness markers, such as *please*?

To what extent are there similarities and differences in the two formulations?

Summary

In this chapter we have looked at selected language-oriented studies that have used methods such as genre analysis, discourse analysis, conversation analysis, speech act theory and politeness theory to analyze and describe spoken Business English. We introduced three genres of business talk, namely meetings, negotiations, and (call centre) service encounters. We have seen what insights discourse-based studies can provide into the structural elements that characterize spoken business genres and the ways in which business professionals communicate in the workplace; i.e. their discourse and verbal interaction patterns. We have considered how the social and organizational context in which a business interaction takes place influences the language and the strategies participants use. We have also discussed ways in which the findings of research based on real language data can be incorporated into teaching Business English. These findings can be used to raise awareness of the characteristics of Business English versus general English and the Business English used in different genres, how contextual factors influence business discourse in different settings, and the variation and similarities in structure and interactional patterns across genres. Finally, the authentic data generated by studies of Business English can be used as a source of realistic Business English for Business English textbooks, and for relevant, real-life materials in the Business English classroom. We will continue to consider spoken Business English in the next chapter when we look at research on intercultural business encounters and consider Business English as a Lingua Franca (see Chapter 2), and the impact of culture and other languages on intercultural communication in meetings and negotiations.

Chapter 4

Intercultural Business Interactions

Introduction

In the previous chapter we introduced a number of spoken forms of Business English, some of the main approaches used to investigate them, and how studies of business talk can inform Business English teaching. In this chapter we consider spoken Business English in the context of international business, drawing on a number of studies of spoken business discourse that focus on how it occurs in intercultural – and multilingual – business encounters. We will see that the presence of intercultural communication in business encounters has become a relevant factor to consider, particularly in relation to teaching Business English as a Lingua Franca and the Business English taught to non-native speakers of English, because doing business increasingly involves contact between people with different linguistic and cultural backgrounds. We focus specifically on meetings and negotiations, which are the most common forms of interaction in international business today, and we consider, in particular, the linguistic and interactional strategies people use for relationship-building, because this is important in interactions in which participants with different cultural backgrounds have to work together. Finally, we suggest how studies of spoken Business English in intercultural encounters can be used in teaching that reflects business talk in the real world.

The importance of research into spoken Business English in intercultural contexts

We saw in Chapter 3 that researchers of spoken Business English base their research on the analysis of corpora of authentic business language or business encounters, using a variety of methods (from discourse analysis to politeness theory) traditionally used in English for Specific Purposes research. A growing number of studies taking this approach have looked at the Business English that is used as a shared code of communication in intercultural encounters. This growth can be explained by two developments. The first is the dramatic growth of English as the most widely used international language for doing business, which has prompted interest in the way English as a Lingua Franca is used in different business genres, interest in the factors that influence its use, and interest in establishing what its characteristics are (see also Chapter 2). The second is that Business English in intercultural contexts has become more relevant, to practitioners as well as teachers, as organizations continue to expand their scope across borders. This has meant that business encounters increasingly involve people with different cultural and linguistic backgrounds. As we discussed in Chapter 2, such encounters may involve interaction between non-native speakers of English only, or between both non-native and native speakers of English.

From the point of view of teaching Business English, it is important to know more about lingua franca Business English as it is used in different spoken and written genres, including the extent to which it differs from the Business English generated by native speakers of English. We noted in Chapter 2 that Business English teaching materials mostly use native-speaker models of English, despite the fact that English is now the most widely used Business Lingua Franca, and despite the fact that more and more people worldwide are learning English as a foreign language. Worldwide, non-native users of English now outnumber native speakers of English (see Graddol, 2006). In Chapter 2 we also discussed the fact that native-like English does not seem to be a criterion for communication success in intercultural encounters. Instead, business competence (i.e. operational know-how) and knowledge of discourse practices in organizations – including genre rules such as how to structure a request letter or chair a meeting – are considered more important than grammatical correctness, idiomaticity, and native-like fluency in Business English, at least according to the Business English as a Lingua Franca speakers who use it with other non-native speakers of English (see Kankaanranta & Planken, 2010). This suggests that a Business English as a Lingua Franca model may now be more appropriate and relevant for teaching Business English than a native-speaker model (see Graddol, 2006). The issue of what should be used as the normative model in teaching has been debated for a number of years. We return to this point in Part V when we reconsider the usefulness and relevance of the native-speaker model for teaching aimed at non-native users of English, not only with respect to developing teaching materials and curricula but also in relation to setting learning targets and proficiency testing.

From intercultural misunderstanding to strategies that work

Although Business English as a Lingua Franca has received increasing interest from researchers in recent years, it is still a fairly new area of business discourse research (see Bargiela-Chiapinni et al., 2013; Koester, 2006). As a result, studies of spoken Business English as a Lingua Franca remain rare. Examples include

Louhiala-Salminen and colleagues' (2005) investigation into the effects of introducing English as the corporate language in two Scandinavian mergers (introduced in Chapter 2), the work of Gina Poncini and Pamela Rogerson-Revell on multicultural European meetings (Poncini, 2002, 2004; Rogerson-Revell, 2010), and the study of intercultural sales negotiations by Brigitte Planken (2005). We will discuss the work of the latter three researchers in more detail below. Poncini and Rogerson-Revell's studies focus on multi-party group interactions, and on what actually happens in such interactions that allows business people from various cultures to work together. Poncini in particular shows how Business English as a Lingua Franca is used not only to achieve transactional, work-related goals, but also to promote cohesion and group feeling among participants with a variety of nationalities. As Holmes and Stubbe (2003) showed the role of relational communication in meetings between native speakers of English, Poncini shows that relational communication is an integral and essential aspect of intercultural business encounters. It lays the groundwork and smooths transactional communication (i.e. task-related communication), and can help to bridge sociocultural differences. The importance of relational strategies in intercultural encounters is confirmed by Planken's (2005) study, in which she looked at the linguistic strategies that negotiators use in Business English as a Lingua Franca in order to achieve rapport. The focus of Pamela Rogerson-Revell's (2010) study is on accommodation strategies, namely the linguistic and interactional strategies non-native – as well as native – speakers of English use in international meetings to promote communicative efficiency. The interest in strategies to achieve relational and transactional goals, rather than the problems and difficulties generally associated with intercultural communication, reflects an important hallmark of more recent investigations of spoken Business English as a Lingua Franca whose aim has been to determine what works in lingua franca communication, rather than to describe what goes wrong.

Relational strategies in multicultural meetings

For her 2002 study, Poncini gained access to a series of multiparty meetings between an Italian multinational and its international distributors. She recorded and observed the meetings, which represented large interactions with up to three dozen participants at a time from 14 different cultures in Asia, Europe, and North America. The study was longitudinal (i.e. conducted over time), because Poncini wanted to examine how the relationship between the company and its distributors evolved and how this was reflected in changes in the discourse over a period of time. Business English as a Lingua Franca was used as the common communication code in all of the meetings. At times, however, participants might switch to other shared (first) languages for asides to those sitting next to them or to confer in smaller groups. In other words, the meetings were multilingual as well as multicultural, which is indeed a common feature of business meetings that involve speakers with multiple first languages.

Poncini looked at three aspects of multilingual business meetings. She examined how language use in multicultural meetings where English is the lingua franca relates to the context (i.e. to roles, relationships, and common goals), and how participants use language to create group feeling and identity. In addition, she investigated how language use (i.e. specific strategies) helps to facilitate communication in intercultural interactions where participants may have different skill levels in Business English as a Lingua Franca and may not always feel at ease using a lingua franca (Poncini, 2002). Poncini takes a pragmatic approach to tackling the question of how to define culture in relation to the context in which the meetings took place, where the context is characterized by multiple nationalities and sociocultural backgrounds. She simply regards the meetings as having a culture or dynamic of their own, co-constructed by the participants over time, for their specific group and their specific constellation of cultural backgrounds.

Poncini looked at a number of the linguistic aspects of Business English as a Lingua Franca, and we deal with three of them here. First, Poncini looked at the use of personal pronouns (we, you, I, etc.). Pronoun use shows how speakers want to present themselves and how they relate to others. For example, an 'I-perspective' might indicate independence and autonomy, while a 'we-perspective' suggests groupness and cooperativeness. An analysis of pronoun use can therefore shed light on the way speakers see and present themselves in relation to others and within the business relationship. We will see later in this chapter that Planken used a similar approach in her study of intercultural negotiations. Second, Poncini examined the use of specialized lexis (vocabulary and phrases that are specific to the company, products, or business context, etc.) as indicators of shared knowledge, professional relationship, and in-group identity. As we saw in the previous chapter, specialist lexis is a characteristic feature of business talk in general. By using specialized lexis, speakers claim a professional identity, and its shared use amongst participants signals that they belong to the same professional community. Third, Poncini looked at participants' use of evaluative lexis (words and phrases such as *good, bad, excellent, success, that was really hard*), which can be used to qualify people, actions, proposals, etc., as either positive or negative. Speakers' use of evaluative lexis can therefore indicate their position, stance, or viewpoint (Poncini, 2002).

Poncini's work provides examples of several interesting ways in which speakers use pronouns to enforce group identity and reflect cooperativeness in intercultural settings. The excerpt that follows, for example, shows how pronoun use, and particularly a clustering of *you* and inclusive *we*, emphasizes the cooperative relationship between participants. The participants are discussing an advertisement for a promotional campaign and its translation from Italian to other languages. Note that (.) indicates a pause of 0.3 seconds or less and (+) a pause between 0.4 and 0.7 seconds.

1	Speaker 1:	do you have that in different languages?
2	Speaker 2:	*we* don't have (.) in a different languages
3		*we* have just for Italy (+)
4		but there is a possibility to get the (.) how do you say (.) the printings (.) in Italian
5		*you* can substitute (+) the (.) only the (.) black (.) text (+) in your language (+)
6		*we* we can send *you* the CD-ROM (+) all the (.) pictures (+)
7		then *you* substitute (.) in-only the text in your languages
8		so *you* translate by yourself
9		it's better because ((she laughs)) *you* know better the language in your country

(Poncini, 2002, p. 359)

Poncini explains that the excerpt illustrates how Speaker 2's alternating use of the personal pronouns *you* and *we* allows her to express the reciprocity of the relationship between her and Speaker 1 (a distributor for Central and South America), reinforcing the idea of cooperativeness at the same time. Poncini regards this as a prerequisite for transactional communication; that is, doing the actual work-related tasks in meetings. In a similar way, Poncini demonstrates how personal pronouns are used to promote a feeling of group identity and solidarity among participants. Again, by indicating solidarity in the language strategies they use, speakers are essentially paving the way for working together on work tasks.

With respect to specialized lexis, Poncini shows that participants use it not only to signal their professional roles in meetings and the company as a whole, but also to frame the business activities that need to be undertaken by the group. For example, in her study specialized lexis was used to express shared expert knowledge about the business at hand, thereby building common ground between participants. Poncini suggests that again this can be taken as a relational strategy aimed at supporting the work the group needs to undertake together. Evaluative lexis, on the other hand, was used primarily for positive image building, in particular by evoking positive associations with the work undertaken by the group or achievements in the organization, etc., all of which promotes a positive feeling about the group. This leads Poncini to conclude that the use of evaluative lexis is also highly relevant as a strategy in interpersonal meeting tasks, particularly to foster positive relationships.

The following is an example from her data. Here, (.) indicates a pause of 0.3 seconds or less, (+) a pause between 0.4 and 0.7 seconds, and (++) a pause between 0.8 and 1.7 seconds.

```
1  Speaker 1:    we had a very good (++) exposure (+)
2                 we get a lot of uh (+) medals (+) with our racers (.)
3                 so (+) was a very good (+) result so of course (+)
                  today the product
4                 it's o-it's perfect (+) let's say (++)
```
                                                    (Poncini, 2002, p. 361)

Poncini's work shows that participants use a range of strategies to build common ground, suggest cooperativeness, and build group identity. The findings are useful from a Business English teaching perspective in that they provide insights into the ways in which meeting participants and negotiators use Business English as a Lingua Franca strategically, to build relationships in intercultural interactions. They also highlight some of the aspects of Business English as a Lingua Franca discourse that contribute to creating the 'groupness' (i.e. shared culture) that is a prerequisite for establishing a good working relationship in multi-party, intercultural encounters. These insights could all be used as starting points for raising awareness among students. Excerpts of data from these studies could be presented in a classroom situation as illustrations of the ways in which different strategies are manifested. The examples could form the basis of a class discussion in which the contextual factors that influence the discourse can be considered explicitly, and can provide an explanation for the strategies that participants use in specific meetings.

When we discuss the teaching of Business English in more detail in Part V, we will see that many current textbooks and teaching materials do relatively little to sensitize students to the impact of sociocultural variables on spoken (or written) Business English. Raising students' awareness of such factors and how they influence language and behaviour in business interactions, particularly in intercultural contexts, is essential if we are to prepare them adequately for what happens in real life. To begin with, however, teaching should at least focus on sensitizing students to the difference between transactional and relational communication, and to the importance of relational communication as a prerequisite for successful transactional communication (see Koester, 2006).

Facework strategies in intercultural negotiations

In her 2005 publication, Planken examines Business English as a Lingua Franca in intercultural sales negotiations, and how participants use 'facework' to manage their relationship across cultures. Facework comprises linguistic strategies (e.g. politeness), non-verbal strategies (e.g. gesturing), and interactional strategies (e.g. turntaking) that speakers use to signal a concern for the 'face' of the hearer; that is, the hearer's need to be liked and respected (Brown & Levinson, 1987). Facework strategies can therefore be said to be inherently relational in nature. Planken compared two corpora of Business English as a Lingua Franca produced in simulated sales negotiations. One corpus consisted of lingua franca examples produced by 14 professional negotiators with between five and 30 years of experience in conducting intercultural negotiations. The other corpus contained lingua franca examples produced by ten students of international business communication with relatively little negotiating experience; that is, pre-experience negotiators. The lingua franca speakers had a variety of cultural backgrounds including French, Italian, and Dutch. Because Planken specifically wanted to examine how the factor 'experience' (in negotiating) influenced participants' use of relational strategies, the negotiations were held in the form of a simulation game. In this way, other factors that could have an influence on the discourse produced – such as topic and size of the deal – could be more easily controlled. Using the game scenario ensured, for example, that the context did not vary with respect to the central proposition being negotiated (the sale of three products), the types of product, and the pricing scheme, etc.

Planken used Spencer-Oatey's model of rapport management (Spencer-Oatey, 2000) as a framework for her analysis. The model offers an approach that is sensitive to issues of face and interpersonal perceptions and assumptions, and how these may impact intercultural communication. According to Spencer-Oatey, rapport or "harmony-disharmony" can be managed across five interaction domains:

1   the domain of speech acts (e.g. requests or refusals)
2   the discourse content domain (e.g. choice of topic, sequencing, etc.)
3   the participation domain (e.g. turntaking, inclusion or exclusion of participants)
4   the stylistic domain (choice of tone, formality level, etc.)
5   the non-verbal domain (e.g. gaze, posture, gestures).

Because it regards rapport on a continuum (from low to high), the model can potentially account for different aspects of relational talk, ranging from politeness and accommodation strategies at the high end of the scale to hostile and conflictive strategies at the low end of the scale. The emphasis in Spencer-Oatey's approach is on identifying the strategies participants use to be able to work together despite differences in their cultural backgrounds, not on pinpointing problematic interaction or miscommunication. Thus, the overarching approach fits not only the focus on communication strategies in lingua franca interaction, as in Planken's study, but also Poncini's focus on relationship management in multi-party meetings (see earlier), and the work of Rogerson-Revell (2007) on accommodation strategies that facilitate international collaboration in meetings, which we discuss later.

Planken focused on two aspects of Business English as a Lingua Franca in negotiations, reflecting two aspects of the rapport management model. The first was negotiators' use of safe topics; that is, topics not directly related to or relevant for the primary goal of the negotiation, which was the pricing of three products (the discourse content domain). The eight topic categories she distinguished included "Initiator" (e.g. greeting, enquiry after well-being, personal introduction, personal work history), "Business environment" (e.g. markets, target groups, competitors, the economy), "Corporate information" (e.g. company history, core activities, distribution, promotion), and "Non-business" (e.g. travel, sports, news, culture, language, family) (2005, p. 386).

The second aspect Planken looked at was the negotiators' use of personal pronouns as indicators of the negotiator relationship. Planken regarded *you* as an indicator of other-orientedness (i.e. concern for the hearer's interests) and inclusive *we* as an indicator of solidarity. Therefore, both *you* and inclusive *we* can signal cooperativeness. In contrast, she regarded the use of exclusive, institutional *we* (i.e. company *we*) as an indicator of professional identity, and the use of *I* as an indicator of self-orientedness (2005, pp. 383–84), and both as distancing devices or indicators of professional face (see Charles (1996), discussed in Chapter 3, who observed similar linguistic tactics in British negotiations).

Planken's analysis highlights clear differences between the discourse of the experienced and pre-experience negotiators. They differed in the categories of safe talk they selected, and the frequency with which they did so. For example, the experienced negotiators initiated a significantly higher number of safe talk topics than the aspiring negotiators, and they initiated safe topics in all three phases of their negotiations; that is, in the opening, bargaining, and closing phases. In contrast, the inexperienced negotiators initiated safe topics in the opening and closing phases only, and they introduced fewer categories of safe talk than the experienced negotiators. While the non-business category of safe talk was used only infrequently in both corpora, it was interesting that the majority of the examples initiated in this category (mostly by the experienced negotiators) referred to the intercultural nature of the negotiations. For example, they involved brief episodes of talk about experiences with the other party's culture, foreign language difficulties, unique cultural characteristics (of the speaker's own culture or the counterpart's culture), and crosscultural comparisons. This suggests that in an intercultural setting, interculturality and cultural difference become resources for safe talk and a means to build the business relationship across cultures, rather than sources of difficulty or relational distance.

Task 4.1 Small talk and safe topics

Think about small talk topics in your country. Are the following topics appropriate? Sports; your job; your salary; your family; holidays; your hobbies; politics; the weather; religion; food; embarrassing experiences you've had.

Which topics would you introduce in a business context to make small talk?

Are these topics different from or similar to the topics you would introduce to make small talk in everyday, non-business contexts?

Now consider the above topics in an intercultural business context. Would they be appropriate or not? What factors do you think this depends on?

Planken also found differences between the two corpora when she looked at the use of personal pronouns, reflecting the degree of solidarity and involvement in the interaction. The most interesting example was the fact that the inexperienced negotiators underused institutional or company *we* in the bargaining phase compared to the experienced negotiators, who used it almost exclusively in transactional communication in this phase. Instead, the inexperienced negotiators' discourse in the bargaining phase mostly featured *I* and *you*, which meant that they communicated in a divisive way rather than by using an inclusive strategy that would make the other party in the negotiation feel as if they were part of a discussion. According to Planken, this created "highly subjective discourse in potentially the most conflictive and face-threatening negotiation phase, [...] suggesting hostility rather than reflecting the no-nonsense, businesslike approach that they might have been aiming for" (2005, p. 396). The contexts in which *you* and *I* were used also differed across negotiator groups. For example, the experienced negotiators would often (re)frame their suggestions from the other person's perspective (the *you* perspective) in order to emphasize the benefits for the hearer; for example, *"If you were to take this offer on the backpacks this time, your management would surely be happy. It really is the best solution for you"* (Planken, 2005, p. 395). The less experienced negotiators also used *you* in suggestions, but often formulated their suggestions as imperatives. This combination made what they said extremely direct (and thus face-threatening); for example, *"You will have to give me ten on that product"* (Planken, 2005, p. 395). The experienced negotiators tended to make greater use of exclusive *we* (i.e. company *we*) or impersonal formulations in such contexts, for instance, *"We would have to say no and go up on the backpacks then"* or *"In that case, prices are simply too high"* (Planken, 2005, p. 395).

The findings of this study are useful from the perspective of Business English teaching because they pinpoint differences between the language behaviour of experienced negotiators and the language behaviour of pre-experience negotiators (i.e. students of Business English). The differences between the two groups not only provide evidence that the amount of experience business people have is a contextual factor that influences what they say in negotiations, but also, and perhaps more importantly, that lack of experience is reflected in students' inappropriate use of certain strategies and is therefore potentially harmful to the business relationship. The study pinpoints a number of areas of relational communication that students need to be sensitized to in order to prepare them for real-life intercultural encounters. For instance, the findings suggest that students should be made aware of safe topics and small talk as a resource for building rapport, and also of the categories of topics that are considered safe. They could benefit from being sensitized to the implications of their inadequate or inappropriate use of personal pronouns, and the implications of formulating potentially face-threatening discourse (i.e. bargaining sequences) from an inappropriately subjective perspective. With respect to specific strategies, students could be prompted to consider the ways in which they can contribute to or threaten the business relationship in a negotiation through personal pronoun use.

More generally, Spencer-Oatey's (2000) rapport management model, with its emphasis on relational communication and strategies for successful intercultural communication, offers a positive and inclusive perspective on doing business across cultures as it considers business to be not just a competitive undertaking, but also a collaborative one. From a pedagogical perspective, this model can provide a useful starting point for Business English as a Lingua Franca teaching geared to skills training in spoken business interactions, as it can raise students' awareness of what they need to take into account in interactions in intercultural relationship-building. Also, as it distinguishes discrete areas of interaction that teaching materials can focus on, the model offers a framework for dealing with various aspects of the interaction in a systematic way.

Accommodation strategies in international meetings

In Chapter 2, we noted that it is important, particularly in relation to teaching Business English, to distinguish contexts in which Business English as a Lingua Franca is used (i.e. amongst speakers whose first language is not English) from contexts in which International Business English is used. As we explained, the latter refers to encounters involving both non-native and native speakers of English. We noted that the presence of native speakers of English in intercultural encounters can potentially cause more problems for the people involved because native speakers may use more complex language and a wider range of vocabulary, for example, which could make them difficult to understand (see Charles & Marschan-Piekkari, 2002, Chapter 2).

Rogerson-Revell's (2010) study on speech accommodation in international, multi-party meetings is relevant for our discussion because it examines encounters in which International Business English is used, and because it also considers the role native as well as non-native speakers play in such interactions. As was the case in the other studies we have discussed in this chapter, Rogerson-Revell's analysis was based on authentic language data. She gained access to a number of meetings held at the annual event of the European branch of the International Actuarian Association, which has representatives in 30 countries. The three meetings she analyzed involved between 21 and 44 participants from various EU countries and a mix of native and non-native speakers of English. The 2010 study builds on an earlier survey conducted by Rogerson-Revell at the same organization after it became concerned about the "unequal participation" in meetings of members whose first language was not English (Rogerson-Revell, 2008, p. 341). The survey investigated meeting participants' perceptions of having to use English in meetings and revealed a range of communication issues and frustrations – particularly from non-native speakers of English – about the difficulties associated with communicating in the international meetings. For example, only around a quarter of the non-native speakers reported feeling comfortable using Business English in the meetings, and they also reported that they would sometimes stay silent because they felt they would not be able to present points in a sufficiently nuanced way, or because they felt they were not competent enough to interrupt other speakers or to claim the floor in a meeting. At the same time, the survey results showed that native speakers in particular felt that they should modify their language use to accommodate the language difference (i.e. the proficiency difference) between them and non-native speakers. According to Rogerson-Revell, this reflects at least an awareness of the impact their 'nativeness' can have on intercultural interactions. The non-native speakers too, felt that linguistic difference between natives and non-natives in the meetings should be accommodated. However, their responses suggest that they felt native speakers did not always make enough effort to adapt their speech to non-native competency levels (Rogerson-Revell, 2008).

Rogerson-Revell (2010) reports specifically on the strategies native and non-native participants used to accommodate linguistic difference and difficulties – i.e. to promote communication efficiency – in the international meetings she analyzed. She used a multi-method approach, using analysis and observation of the three meetings together with information from the earlier survey of participants to identify two types of accommodation strategies: normalization strategies and convergence strategies.

The use of normalization strategies was first noted by Firth (1996) in lingua franca telephone negotiations. Firth observed that participants do their very best to understand one another at all times and use a range of conversational strategies to make intercultural interaction seem unproblematic and comprehensible "in the face of extraordinary, deviant, and sometimes 'abnormal' linguistic behaviour" (Firth, 1996, p. 237). Rogerson-Revell's (2010) analysis showed that participants used different normalization strategies, such as "let it pass" and "make linguistic difference explicit" in the meetings (pp. 442, 444). In the case of the first, "let it pass", participants simply ignore (that is, tolerate) ambiguous or idiosyncratic language as long as what is being said is understandable in the context. In other words, the form of a message is regarded as less important than its content. By choosing not to focus on deviations from 'normality', speakers show solidarity and acceptance of difference, which is positive for the working relationship. More importantly, they keep the interaction going. The second normalization strategy, "make linguistic difference explicit", involves participants explicitly requesting clarification or explanation, for example, in reaction to 'abnormal' language usage. Native speakers might ask for explicit clarification in situations where the form of a non-native speaker's message deviates from normality so much that its content is not clear, while non-native speakers might ask a native speaker for clarification in situations where the non-native speaker's English competence is insufficient to understand the 'complex' content of the native speaker's message. Another way to explicitly indicate linguistic difference (e.g. unequal levels of competence) is for non-native speakers to code-switch to their first language when they experience word-finding problems.

Two of the convergence strategies Rogerson-Revell (2010) identified in the meetings are "procedural formality" and "careful speech style'" (pp. 446, 449). Procedural formality strategies are interactional, and were most clearly reflected in participants' efforts to keep to the procedural rules of formal meetings, with respect to, for example, turntaking procedures and following the agenda. In the meetings, participants rarely self-selected a turn to speak but waited instead for formal speaker invitations from the chairperson. Also, the chairpersons did their best to maintain order and progress chronologically through the points on the agenda. These strategies allow participants to keep to the genre rules, and with that, they promote the overall orderliness of the meetings. Rogerson-Revell suggests that procedural strategies help accommodate non-native participants from various cultures (potentially with other ways of 'doing' meetings) by clarifying the structure and the progress of these specific meetings. They also accommodate non-native participants who may lack the linguistic competence to self-select a turn to speak or to interrupt. As we saw earlier, from their survey responses, it would seem that interrupting and claiming the floor were indeed seen as difficulties by the non-native participants.

The second convergence strategy Rogerson-Revell identified − "careful speech style" − is reflected mainly in native speakers' adapting their speech delivery in different ways (e.g. by speaking deliberately, speaking more slowly, or using very clear pronunciation), and in speakers' avoidance of "high-context communication", that is, idioms or collocations, metaphors, and unusual or archaic vocabulary. The incidence of high-context communication in the meetings Rogerson-Revell looked at was low, and she suggests that this is evidence of the fact that careful speech style was used as an accommodation strategy by participants. The survey responses from the non-natives suggested that they found it hard to understand certain native speakers because of their strong regional accents (e.g. Irish, Scottish), but this is a feature of speech that is more difficult to adapt, and it was unclear from the meetings whether natives accommodated their speech at this level and attempted to modify their accent. Again, however, insights such as these could be used to at least raise awareness among native speakers of English who are involved in intercultural encounters with non-native users of International Business English.

In relation to teaching Business English as a Lingua Franca, some researchers have suggested that in order to improve intercultural business communication, teaching should also focus on native speakers of English involved in intercultural business encounters (see for example Charles & Marschan-Piekkari, 2002). Based on the findings of studies like Rogerson-Revell's, they could be made aware of the impact their native speech has on less proficient counterparts in intercultural encounters − i.e. what it is about their speech that makes them hard to understand for non-native speakers, and the specific difficulties that non-native speakers of English experience when they have to use International Business English in encounters with native speakers. Teaching materials might also be developed that focus on the different types of accommodation strategies that native speakers can use to promote mutual understanding and solve some of the difficulties non-native speakers experience in interactions with native speakers of English.

Task 4.2 Communication strategies

Think back to an intercultural encounter in which you communicated in English as a Lingua Franca, or in International Business English. (See earlier in this chapter for an explanation of the difference between the two.)

Do you remember using any of the accommodation strategies that Rogerson-Revell (2010) identified in her study? Which ones?

To what extent did you feel that the other person in the conversation accommodated their speech to yours?

Did the strategies you (both) used contribute to the efficiency of the encounter? How?

Summary

In this chapter, we have considered Business English in the context of intercultural meetings and negotiations. The research we profiled provides examples of the relational strategies speakers use in such contexts to build positive working relationships, signal cooperativeness among group members, promote group feeling and identity, and build rapport across cultures. We have seen that relational discourse is an important feature of Business English used in intercultural settings, where common ground has to be found between people with different cultural backgrounds. We have seen how relational communication is intertwined with transactional communication in business contexts, and how speakers invest in establishing a cooperative relationship, which is necessary for people to be able to work together. We have also considered the role of native speakers of English in intercultural encounters in International Business English, and discussed some of the accommodation strategies they (and non-native speakers of English) can use in such encounters to make communication between native and non-native speakers of Business English more efficient. Finally, we have suggested how the findings from the studies profiled in this chapter might inform Business English teaching. In the next chapter, we continue this discussion and focus on several studies of spoken business English that have explored how research can be used as the basis for teaching.

Chapter 5

Teaching Spoken Business English

Introduction

In the previous chapter we considered research on Business English in intercultural interactions, including some of the insights it has given us into the nature of Business English as a Lingua Franca, and we reviewed what we know about the linguistic and discursive strategies people use in lingua franca English to reach relational as well as transactional goals in intercultural encounters. We also considered ways in which insights from the studies we profiled might be incorporated into teaching materials for Business English as a Lingua Franca, or for learners who do not speak English as their first language. In this, the final chapter of Part II, we broaden our discussion again and consider the relevance of research on spoken business genres more generally for the teaching of spoken Business English.

While we have noted in earlier chapters that spoken business genres have received greater interest from researchers over the past two decades, the transfer from research to the teaching of spoken Business English has not been as evident as has perhaps been the case for written business genres. We will see in Part III that an important approach to research on written Business English has been to apply genre theory and genre analysis to identify and describe specific text types (i.e. to identify the move structure, the lexicogrammatical realization of those moves, and the communication purpose of the text type) and the context in which they are produced, primarily within academia and business (see Swales, 1990; Bhatia, 1993). We will also see in Part III how genre theory has subsequently had a considerable influence on the way in which Business English writing is taught as it offers a clear three-step framework that can be used to develop teaching materials, to illustrate genres in use, and to highlight variation across genres (see Chapter 6).

Although the notion of genre has certainly played a role in research on spoken Business English too, in the sense that one of the early aims of researchers was to identify the move structure of genres such as negotiations and meetings, we have seen in previous chapters that researchers studying spoken workplace discourse have also used a variety of other linguistic, interactional, and discourse-oriented analyses in addition to genre analysis in order to examine spoken English in business interactions, the factors that influence it, and how Business English allows people to do their jobs. This may be because the more spontaneous language data that is generated in spoken contexts (e.g. in a meeting) shows greater variability and is less predictable (i.e. by nature less ordered and orderly at a micro-level) than language data generated in writing, which usually results from a more planned and deliberate process and may have involved a lengthy revision process. The fact that spoken genres in this sense may appear to be less stable than written genres may mean that they therefore lend themselves less readily to generic description and the matching of form and function that researchers try to do when they take a genre approach (but see Handford's genre approach to business meetings below). Whatever the underlying cause, genre theory has not been as instrumental in translating research findings into teaching practice for spoken Business English as it has been for written Business English.

Bargiela-Chiappini et al. (2013) have noted that unlike studies in English for Specific Purposes, discourse-based studies in general have not been traditionally motivated by pedagogical concerns, or by learners' needs. As a result, they have not always aimed to generate – let alone explicitly offer – suggestions as to how the findings could inform teaching, even though (as we have seen in the previous chapters) insights from such studies can at the very least form the basis for awareness-raising materials for Business English courses (see for example our discussion of Poncini, 2002; 2004, in the previous chapter). In the next section we look at the work of three researchers who have used an English for Specific Purposes approach to analyze spoken business genres because their research aims were (at least partly) pedagogical. They subsequently used their findings to formulate recommendations with respect to teaching and training. We begin by profiling Dow's (1999) study of simulated negotiations, which was conducted when linguistic research on negotiations was still relatively rare. Based on a comparison of student and professional negotiators' discourse, he identifies a number of key areas of difficulty for students and suggests negotiation teaching materials that could be developed to help students deal with them. We then discuss Almut Koester and Michael Handford's work, which is based on quantitative analyses of large corpora of naturally occurring spoken workplace discourse. Koester's research (2006, 2012) on the ABOT corpus incorporates various spoken business genres, while Handford's (2010) study focuses on business meetings from the CANBEC corpus. Both researchers offer recommendations as to how research findings should be incorporated into teaching and training. Koester's work hasin fact generated what remains one of the few examples to date of a truly data-driven English for Specific Business Purposes book for students (Koester, 2004). As we discuss in Part V of this volume, the work Koester and her co-authors did on the *Business Advantage Series* (Koester et al., 2012), has resulted in the publication of one of the few sets of published materials that has begun to address the needs of more advanced learners of Business English.

Ritual exchanges in negotiations

Dow (1999) reports on a study he carried out in the early 1990s in which he compared the Business English use of inexperienced negotiators (students) with experienced negotiators (marketing specialists), all of whom were non-native (Austrian) speakers of English. More specifically, he compared their negotiation performance with respect to a number of interactional and discursive features (e.g. topic control, openings, and closings) and a number of discursive tactics (e.g. politeness and indirect speech acts) using methods from discourse analysis and conversation analysis. Although the scope of the study was limited, in that it was based on a corpus of only three simulated negotiations, we discuss it here because it is a rare example of an investigation that, like Planken's study of facework strategies in negotiations (see Chapter 4), considers the influence of professional business experience on language use. Dow's study is interesting in relation to teaching Business English not only because it identifies areas that are potentially problematic for inexperienced negotiators, but also because it aimed to test the usefulness of the approach taken in a specific textbook, *Negotiate in English* (Lees, 1983), that was widely used in Business English classrooms at the time, and the effectiveness of the negotiation simulation game (Swedish Wood) that featured in the textbook. Dow collected the data for his study on the basis of this negotiation simulation game, recording two experienced business people and four inexperienced Business English students as they conducted the Swedish Wood negotiation and using that recording for his analysis. This allowed him not only to investigate Business English in negotiations, but also to determine to what extent the textbook dealt with any of the problems relating to the inexperienced negotiators' competence (or lack of it) that emerged from his comparative analysis.

Overall, Dow's analysis showed that the students conducted topic transactions, openings and closings, and tactful and polite bargaining less effectively, and often inappropriately, in comparison to the experienced negotiators. With respect to topic control, for instance – i.e. the ability of a speaker to not only initiate topics but also to recognize the transaction boundaries of topics (e.g. to know when the other party signals that a topic is closed), and to react appropriately (i.e. signal acknowledgement) when the transaction from one topic to the next is made – Dow found that the inexperienced negotiators were less able than the experienced negotiators to recognize topic boundaries. This was signalled by the fact that when they did acknowledge closure of a topic, their language displayed greater hesitation and tentativeness than that of the experienced negotiators (e.g. "*Hm mm*", "*well, yeah*", Dow, 1999, p. 85), as well as by the fact that in a number of instances in the corpus the inexperienced negotiators did not acknowledge the closure of a topic (by the other negotiator) at all, but remained quiet in the next turn. In contrast, the experienced negotiators always acknowledged topic closure and consistently used an enthusiastic endorsement to do so (e.g. *"good, that sounds acceptable"*, *"great"*, or *"you will have a lovely time"*, Dow, 1999, p. 86).

A second difference that Dow identified relates to the student negotiators' difficulties in producing appropriate responses in adjacency pairs; that is, paired sets of responses such as question-answer or invitation-acceptance. Dow notes that such pairs of responses are what is expected in terms of linguistic behaviour – i.e. what is seen as the norm in certain contexts – such that, in the case of question-answer, for example, an answer is expected to follow the question in the turn that immediately follows it. If the preferred or expected response to a first part of a pair is not given, the alternative, dispreferred response needs to be formulated politely, or mitigated. In a negotiation context, for example, an offer may be followed by the preferred response – i.e. acceptance – or by the dispreferred response – i.e. mitigated rejection. This would comply with the norms, and therefore what people are expecting in a negotiation context. Dow found that student negotiators often flouted the norms for adjacency pairs, whereas experienced negotiators hardly ever did. Inexperienced negotiators would readily produce dispreferred responses in contexts where an experienced negotiator would rarely do so, and they would formulate dispreferred responses with little or no mitigation or linguistic politeness (e.g. "I think we should talk about arranging a fixed rate + *I don't*" [= request + unmitigated refusal], "So what do you suggest? What do we do now? + *One point I can't understand if you are honest*" [= question + no answer / accusation], Dow, 1999, p. 91). Overall, Dow notes that the inexperienced negotiators showed a lack of appreciation of politeness strategies in that they were unable to formulate face-threatening speech acts indirectly, and they failed to include even common mitigating strategies such as hedges. Like Planken (2005), Dow observed that the students had significant problems in the area of small talk (i.e. relational talk) and in applying appropriate facework (i.e. politeness strategies) in the bargaining phase of negotiations.

A third difference Dow observed relates to the way in which the two sets of negotiators exchanged openings. Conversational analysts have identified the ritual exchange (i.e. the expected, usual way of doing things) for openings, which Dow explains using the example of Schegloff and Sacks' identification of the essential features of telephone call openings (Schegloff and Sacks, 1973). Openings are realized interactionally as follows:

1 Names are used to address the other party or to call their attention ('greeting' – first part of an adjacency pair);
2 An answer must follow the call for attention and this must be in the next turn ('greeting' – second part of an adjacency pair);
3 A lack of response in this turn (i.e. missing the second part of an adjacency pair) implies a negative response and will be regarded as impolite;

4 Speakers should not only reply positively to questions such as *How are you* ('ask after' – first part of an adjacency pair) but also reciprocate and ask how the other person is doing ('reply + return' – second part of an adjacency pair).

(Dow, 1999, p. 86, slightly adapted)

Dow's experienced negotiators realized their opening sequences as would be expected on the basis of the above (e.g. *"Hello Mr S., nice to meet you again"* + *"Good morning, Mr D."* and *"How are you doing?"* + *"Fine, how about yourself?"*, Dow, 1999, p. 87). In contrast, in the opening sequences of the inexperienced speakers, the responses to the first turn were either missing (e.g. *"Good morning Sir, I'm M.P. + X"*), or they were inappropriate, both of which suggested impoliteness on the part of the speaker from whom a response was expected (e.g. *"Hello Mr R, how are you?"* + *"Not as good as we have seen us for the first time"* [= failure to respond with a reciprocal enquiry after well-being + insertion of dispreferred second pair part instead], Dow, 1999, p. 87).

The inappropriately formulated ritual exchanges Dow observed in the student negotiators' Business English discourse, their limited grasp of resources to express tact and politeness, and their awkwardness in relational exchanges (i.e. using safe talk or talk on neutral topics, unrelated to the business task at hand) clearly signal potential problem areas for learners of Business English that, as Dow suggests, could be significantly reduced if students were to receive "more narrowly focused linguistic training" in these areas (Dow, 1999, p. 84). Interestingly, Dow notes that the negotiation textbook from which the simulation game used for the study was taken did not sufficiently accommodate students' needs with respect to the problem areas he identified, because "it does not pay enough attention to the interactional dimension of language, which may be critical in setting the tone of a business negotiation", and because it is "too restricted in its view of language which sees e.g. 'the threat' as a single phrase functional exponent which can be drilled, thereby oversimplifying the remarkably complex phenomenon of indirection in English politeness exchanges" (Dow, 1999, p. 97). This last comment in particular would still seem to be relevant in relation to Business English teaching materials today, as it was also found to be the case in a very recent study by Lam et al. (2014), who aimed to evaluate the teaching and learning resources used within the Business English module offered in the English as a second language programme at Hong Kong Polytechnic University. Lam et al. note that "like in most business English textbooks", the examples that were presented in the materials to illustrate certain discourse functions were largely "decontextualized" (that is, presented without any information about the context in which they were produced), and were often presented in terms of isolated sentences, such that 'disagreement', for example, might be exemplified by a single utterance *"That's not what I meant"*, without any further explanation or explicit discussion of "how the examples achieve what they want to achieve" (Lam et al., 2014, p. 74). They make the point that without any discussion of the linguistic and situational context in which an example is produced, it is extremely hard to assess whether an utterance is pragmatically appropriate or suitable for use in a particular context. Similar observations about the lack of "sociocultural contextualization" of Business English examples presented in textbooks and teaching resources have been made by Williams (1988), whose study we referred to in Chapter 1 of this volume, and by Koester (2002), specifically in relation to the way in which the language of meetings is presented to students in textbooks. We return to this point, and to a more detailed discussion of Lam et al.'s study, in Chapter 12.

One of the recommendations Dow formulates to address the need for more varied and complex contextualized examples is that teaching materials should incorporate a greater variety of examples of "formulaic responses (other than only the standard greeting-greeting adjacency pairs)" as this "would increase the range of students' discourse in critical interactional phases" (Dow, 1999, p. 98). Such materials should also include exercises that encourage students to inter-actively produce ritual exchanges and a variety of responses in a range of adjacency pairs. He recommends that "information-gap type exercises" should be developed that involve, for example, "question-answer, inform-acknowledge exchanges […], request-grant, accuse-excuse, assess-agree" (Dow, 1999, p. 98). In this way, students are exposed to a broad range of examples and a variety of linguistic realizations for a particular function, which would also raise their awareness and encourage them to decide whether the examples presented to them are appropriate or not, and the factors that determine this. This could form the basis for further class discussion and extended practice, for example, on the basis of longer roleplays that would allow students to produce longer stretches of sustained interaction. In Chapter 8, we will look at a study by Gimenez (2014) on computer-mediated communication that also considers how this type of extended roleplaying, combined with awareness-raising exercises, can be incorporated into the Business English classroom.

Finally, Dow recommends that materials should incorporate a more extensive focus on "the peculiarities of English politeness formula such as hedges […], and features of mitigation" (Dow, 1999, p. 98). Also, and like Planken (2005), he recommends that materials should be designed so as to train students to incorporate small talk and relational discourse in the opening and closing phases of negotiations more efficiently and effectively, as this would seem to be a particularly problematic area for them.

Task 5.1 Designing a Business English session on negotiation

Prepare a two-hour lesson on negotiation for a group of students, i.e. inex-perienced negotiators, who are non-native speakers of English. Using the insights from Dow's study (discussed in this chapter) and/or Planken's study (see Chapter 4), decide on a specific language and/or skills focus for the two-hour session, formulate a learning objective/learning objectives, and develop a lesson plan. As part of the plan, design at least two classroom activities and a self-study assignment. Give reasons for your ideas for the lesson and the activities.

Essential language in business meetings

Handford's (2010) study reports on an extensive and detailed analysis of the language and communication practices people employ in business meetings. The corpus used for the study consisted of 64 business meetings from the Cambridge and Nottingham Business English Corpus (CANBEC) and comprised nearly a million words. The business meetings were generated in 26 companies (in the UK, elsewhere in Europe, and Japan) and involved 226 speakers from the UK and 35 speakers from other countries, although Handford's analysis focuses primarily on the data produced by native speakers of English. The study is interesting in that it applies Bhatia's most recent insights into genre and discourse in its analysis of meetings (Bhatia, 2004). What makes the study exceptional is that genre analysis has been mainly associated with research on written professional and academic discourse, as we noted earlier in this chapter. Handford's research shows how genre analysis can be applied just as productively to spoken business discourse, providing insights into the structure and phases of meetings and the discursive practices that occur within each, and into a variety of discursive features such as keywords and concordances (i.e. words that go together, such as *business* + *meeting*), word clusters, interpersonal language, and turn-taking. In doing so, Handford analyzes meetings at multiple levels of interaction and provides authentic examples of language use throughout to illustrate his findings. The study is particularly illuminating because it identifies, on the basis of frequency counts, the language and discursive features that characterize the genre of meetings, the impact of context on those features, and the frequency of certain discursive practices in different types of meetings. The study can therefore be useful for teaching and training, because it identifies the language that is essential in meetings – the language that makes a meeting a meeting – and because it presents and discusses the corpus data in relation to the broader professional and social context in which they were generated. It therefore provides us with the type of contextualized examples that would seem to be lacking in many current teaching resources (see earlier in this chapter and also Chapter 12).

Handford offers a number of recommendations as to how the study's findings can be incorporated into teaching. For example, he concludes that the language of the CANBEC meetings he analyzed can be grouped into four overarching functions or purposes: 1) procedure-focusing, 2) information-focusing, 3) decision-focusing, and 4) negotiating-focusing (Handford, 2010). He further suggests that each of these should be regarded for teaching purposes as essential higher-level meeting skills which can be broken down into several lower-level skills. For example, with regard to procedure-focusing, he identifies the sub-skills of "clarifying what you have said", "clarifying what your interlocutor has said", "clarifying your general position", "asking for clarification", and "summarizing effectively", while with respect to decision-making and problem-solving, he notes "raising an issue", "discussing an issue", "discussing solutions", "reaching consensus", and "postponing or evading decisions" (Handford, 2010, p. 255). Teaching materials and exercises should be developed that specifically train these lower-level skills sets, so that learners of Business English can develop competency in performing all four of the overarching skills. Furthermore, and this supports the findings of several studies that we discussed elsewhere in Part II, Handford recommends that the interpersonal aspects of communication in meetings, such as building business relationships and attention to face and politeness strategies, should be given greater attention in Business English courses than they are now, as his analyses show that relational communication is an essential part of business meetings (see also Charles 1996; Dow, 1999; Poncini, 2002; Koester, 2006, 2012; Planken, 2005).

In addition, Handford notes that although metaphors and idioms are not among the most frequent word combinations that he found in the corpus, they do play a distinctive discursive role in meetings, particularly by powerful people, for example in evaluating participation in the meeting (e.g. *"I'm completely lost"* (p. 258), which implies that confusion has been created because the other speaker has not been clear). He suggests that metaphors and idioms tend to be neglected in teaching and in teaching materials, and that this is unfortunate because it puts Business English learners "at a pragmatic disadvantage when it comes to dealing with real business people in real situations and to using language that is 'in harmony' with the community of practice" (Handford, 2010, p. 258). He subsequently presents a sample exercise on this specific topic, in which learners are first asked to consider a list of metaphors and idioms from the corpus (e.g. *your letter has found its way to me, dive in, grab a chair, I'm in the dark, it's not rocket science, you're clear where we're coming from*) and are then asked to decide whether they consider their use (in the context of a business meeting) as "conflictual", "neutral" or "friendly" (Handford, 2010, p. 258). Learners are then asked to consider how the metaphors and idioms they view as conflictual could be communicated in a less contentious way, and to practise these linguistic alternatives with a fellow learner. Finally, learners are asked to answer a number of questions that allow them to consider and locate the idioms and metaphors in a wider context of use. These questions include: Would you be comfortable using this type of language at work? Do you want to use conflictual language at work? What are the dangers, and what are the potential benefits? (Handford, 2010, p. 258). This type of exercise allows learners not only to practise the language of meetings, but also encourages them to link language use to context and to assess how particular language features would be viewed in their own community of practice (i.e. at work) or in their own culture. Similar materials could be developed relatively easily with a focus on many of the other discursive features and lexicogrammatical features of meetings in English that Handford identifies.

The key characteristics of workplace discourse

We end this chapter with a discussion of the genre-based work of Koester (2006, 2012) on the ABOT corpus, which comprises around 35,000 words of formal and informal spoken interaction in a wide variety of workplace contexts. The data for the corpus was recorded in eight organizations in Britain and the US and generated by speakers of the two main varieties of English, British, and American English (see also Chapter 3). Koester's central aim was to identify spoken genres that occur across a wide variety of workplace environments, and to examine specific features (e.g. discursive practices and lexicogrammatical features) of those genres and the features that occur across various genres. Koester identified five so-called "unidirectional genres" in the data: 1) briefing, 2) service encounter, 3) procedural and directive discourse, 4) requesting action / permission / goods, and 5) reporting, and three so-called "collaborative genres": 1) making arrangements, 2) decision-making, and 3) discussing and evaluating (Koester, 2006, pp. 32–33). All of these genres are regarded by Koester as "transactional" (or work-based) in nature. In addition, she identified two further genres in the corpus: 1) office gossip and 2) small talk, which she classifies as "non-transactional", or relational (Koester, 2006, p. 33). The key differences between the genres Koester identifies show convincingly that genre is indeed an important factor that influences linguistic choices, and shapes workplace discourse. Other factors that are shown to be of influence are power and social distance, and this supports the findings of a number of other discourse-based studies that we have discussed elsewhere in Part II (e.g. Holmes & Stubbe, 2003). Finally, Koester's analyses also show that relational language is an important and integral part of workplace talk. Interestingly, she notes that there is no "sharp distinction between 'on-task' transactional talk and relational talk or small talk" (Koester, 2006, p. 161). In other words, as we have seen in some of the other studies we considered in Part II, relational and transactional language are often intertwined, with even clearly transactional episodes of interaction displaying evidence of relational language strategies (see Poncini, 2002 and Holmes & Stubbe, 2003).

Based on the findings of her study, Koester (2012) suggests that "one of the most important contributions that research can make to teaching and teacher training is to develop an awareness in learners and teachers of the key character- f workplace discourse" (Koester, 2012, p. 150). She points out five key characteristics and recommends that each receives more attention in teaching (and learning):

1 Workplace interactions are different from everyday interactions with respect to goal orientations as well as other aspects such as asymmetry (see Chapter III for a discussion of the differences between everyday talk and workplace talk).

2 There are important differences between the vocabulary and phraseology used in business situations versus social or informal situations, as shown in the different frequencies of certain words or combinations of words in business versus non-business corpora. (See also our discussion of Nelson's (2000, 2006) comparative analyses in Chapter 3.)

3 Because it is primarily goal-oriented, workplace talk is structured, and participants use a variety of (interrelated) genres to realize work-related tasks. (See also Chapter 9, where we discuss the notions of intertextuality and interdiscursivity in detail.)

4 Problem-solving is a key activity in the workplace and a large proportion of workplace discourse is therefore devoted to discussing problems, devising solutions and making evaluations.

5 People who need to work together attend to relational as well as transactional concerns. Relational concerns manifest themselves in the use of various kinds of relational strategies used to realize politeness and facework, for example.

(Koester, 2012, p. 150, slightly adapted).

All of these areas could form the focus of courses or teaching activities for Business English courses. We will return to Koester's work and to specific applications of her research in teaching Business English in Part V of this volume.

Task 5.2 Designing a Business English course on meeting skills

You have been asked to develop a course in Business English for entry-level employees (university graduates) in a multinational company. The course should train managers' meeting skills. The course will be taken by native as well as non-native speakers of English (14 participants in all).

Based on the studies by Handford and Koester (and any other studies in Part II that you think might prove useful), decide which areas you would want to focus on, and explain why.

Next, formulate a learning objective or learning objectives for the course, and explain its/their relevance for the target group.

Finally, create a sample activity or exercise that you could use in class.

Summary

In this chapter, the final chapter of Part II on spoken Business English, we have considered the relevance of research on spoken business genres for the teaching of spoken Business English by profiling three studies whose aims were (partly) pedagogical, and whose findings formed the basis for specific recommendations for teaching and training. In the three chapters that make up Part III of this volume, we will move the focus of our discussion to written genres of business English and consider the influence that research on written genres with an English for Specific Purposes approach has had on teaching Business English.

Part III

Written Business English

Chapter 6

Introducing Written Business English

Introduction

In Part II (Chapters 3, 4, and 5, we looked at how a number of researchers have investigated spoken Business English taking an English for Specific Purposes approach, and how these studies and other language-based studies have influenced how we teach Business English. In the next three chapters, we do the same for written Business English. This chapter introduces the research that has been done on written forms of Business English. It discusses the main approaches that have been taken in the investigation of common business documents such as letters and emails, where the emphasis has been on how such texts are produced, and it begins to discuss how these have also impacted the ways in which people are taught to produce such documents. Chapter 7 continues this discussion and considers the research that has focused on the processes surrounding how business texts are created and interpreted, and Chapter 8 looks specifically at how the most recent research taking an English for Specific Purposes approach has been incorporated into teaching and training focusing on written Business English.

The most influential scholar to have taken an English for Specific Purposes approach focused on written Business English is Vijay Bhatia. This chapter therefore looks first at his work, and then at the work of researchers such as Catherine Nickerson, Leena Louhiala-Salminen, Didar Akar, and Jonathan Gains, who used a similar approach in their pioneering investigations of the forms of written Business English (e.g. fax communication and email) that were commonly used by business organizations at the end of the last century. This work is important because it has helped shape the field of Business English and how written forms of communication have been taught since then. The second part of this chapter discusses the work of scholars like Ulla Connor and Almut Koester, who have re-applied Bhatia's approach to business writing in English with specific reference to teaching.

Vijay Bhatia: A genre approach to written Business English

In 1993, Vijay Bhatia published his influential volume, *Analysing genre: Language in professional settings*. Previous to this, John Swales' work on the analysis of academic texts (Swales, 1990) had effectively established the notion of genre in the field of English for Specific Purposes as a descriptive approach to understanding how written texts are produced and understood by professional writers. In both Swales' work and Bhatia's extension of this work, the aim of the analysis is not to contribute further to any one particular type of theory, but to understand more about how a particular type of text is used by a certain professional community. This is why Business English research that has taken an English for Specific Purposes approach is data-driven – i.e. focused on the analysis of a set of data – and not theory driven. Analysts decide on the most appropriate theory to refer to in their work depending on the type of data that they are looking at, so that they do not rely on only one theory but may use several theories together to provide a thorough understanding of what is happening in the written text or spoken interaction. Both Swales and Bhatia were influenced by the ideas of the cultural anthropologist Clifford Geertz, who talked about the need to take the contexts of actions into account (not just the actions themselves) in order to create a "thick description" of a particular culture (Geertz, 1973). Many studies of written Business English use this idea and aim to produce a "thick description" of texts by trying to understand how they are used in a particular context. In order to do this, researchers study the processes surrounding the creation of the texts and they explore what is happening in the texts at several different levels of analysis. We discuss this in more detail later in this chapter and in Chapter 7, and explain how Bhatia's approach and the work of the researchers who were influenced by him have increased our understanding of how written texts are used in business contexts.

Bhatia extended Swales' work beyond the written texts that are used in the academic world and made reference to other professional contexts with, for instance, the inclusion of both legal texts and business texts. Swales' (1990) account showed that common academic texts such as research articles have a similar communicative purpose and that this leads to a typical structure in the text, which he called a "move structure" that can be identified and reproduced by the scientists who write them. Swales' central idea was that experienced writers know how to make an effective move within a text and that this contributes to the particular communicative purpose of the text and ultimately to its success. Moves analysis is of particular interest in teaching Business English as it divides the text into functional chunks, equivalent to a move, and it then shows how each of these chunks or moves makes a contribution to creating an effective piece of writing. Bhatia built on Swales' ideas about identifying different moves that are typical of specific types of text, and then showed that there are obligatory moves that must be included in a text if it is going to be a text of that type, which he refers to as "discriminative moves", and other optional moves that individual writers may choose to include if they wish, but which do not affect the integrity of the text, which he refers to as "non-discriminative moves". If one or more discriminative moves are absent, then the text under analysis will not be recognized as an example of that text type. For example, if a traditional closing line such as *Yours sincerely* and a reference to a vacancy are both missing from a text, then that text no longer conforms to what we normally associate with an application letter. If a writer fails to incorporate the discriminative moves associated with that type of text then the text is still a text, but the reader will not necessarily recognize what type of text it is, and in all likelihood it will not achieve its communicative purpose. Bhatia also showed how individual writers use different textual choices within a given move in order to create the text, depending on how skilled they are as a creator of that type of text. This explains why some people are better at writing than others, even if they all recognize a particular type of text and know how to write one, and it also suggests that it is possible to teach people how to become better writers if they understand more about the impact of how they write on the person reading their text.

Bhatia's discussion of written business texts identifies three ways in which a text can be analyzed, providing an analysis at three different levels. The first of these is the analysis of the lexicogrammatical features of the text – the words and grammatical structures that are typical of a particular type of text, such as the use of the pronoun *I* in application letters in Western countries, which is what most people reading the text would expect. The second is the text patterns or chunks of text that are typically used in a specific type of text, such as the text chunk *Please do not hesitate to contact me*, which is the realization of a non-discriminative move that signals that the end of a business letter is imminent. It doesn't need to be there for the reader to recognize that the text is a letter, but it often is present and its inclusion may help the text to be more effective. The third level of analysis is the structural organization of a text, which means the combination of discriminative and non-discriminative structural elements or moves which distinguish one type of text from another. In Bhatia's work, where a specific type of text can be identified on the basis of all of these three levels of analysis and a specific communicative purpose can also be identified, it then becomes possible to talk about a special type of text, called a *genre*. People who work in the same community and use the same types of texts every day to accomplish their work recognize and learn to use these special ways of communicating effectively. This is why genre analysis is such a powerful tool in teaching Business English: it shows what a businessperson needs to do at several different levels within the text to be an effective writer and to create a text that achieves its purpose.

As far as business texts are concerned, Bhatia looked specifically at sales and application letters and showed that the fact that letters like this have a similar communicative purpose – i.e. they both promote a product or a person in a positive way and sell that product or person to the reader – predicts that they will also have a similar structure. He placed typical examples of application letters and sales letters side by side and identified the moves within the structure of each one that ran parallel because of the shared communicative purpose. This allowed him to identify seven different moves that were shared in both genres, as follows:

1   Establishing credentials
2   Introducing the offer/candidature

   a Offering the product or service/candidature
   b Essential detailing of the offer/candidature
   c Indicating value of the offer/candidature

3   Offering incentives
4   Enclosing documents
5   Soliciting response
6   Using pressure tactics
7   Ending politely

The analysis showed that both the content of each move and the structure of the genre were important. Bhatia then went on to look at each move in turn to see how it was realized – i.e. the lexis and grammar that were typically used in each one. As we discuss later in this chapter, many researchers in Business English have been influenced by this approach and have replicated Bhatia's work for both these and other written business genres. Genre analysis allows the analyst, and therefore also the teacher, to understand how a text works in terms of content, structure, and overarching purpose.

A further important contribution to the field of English for Specific Purposes in general and Business English in particular was that Bhatia showed that different genres could be realized quite differently from one culture to another, such that US application letters for instance are much longer and contain much more 'sales' information promoting the candidate than their counterparts in South East Asia, which are typically much shorter, and informational rather than promotional. The communicative purpose is the same in each case (i.e. to secure an interview?), but the form and content of the genre is different in the two different regions. Again, this has clear implications for teaching Business English as it identifies what teachers can usefully focus on with their students, not only in the content of a letter (e.g. should it be informational or promotional?), but also in in its structure (e.g. what moves should be included and how should these be realized?). In the next section, we profile the work of several researchers who have applied Bhatia's ideas or a similar approach to the analysis of other forms of written Business English, including documents that have originated in different national and organizational business cultures, and we consider the similarities and differences between them.

Task 6.1 Comparing different genres

Look for an example of an application letter and an example of a sales letter. These can either be in English or in your own language.

> Put them side by side and see if you can find any of the moves that Bhatia (1993) identified.
>
> Decide if there are any differences between the two texts. Do you think these texts are structured or realized differently in your own language than they are in English?

The influence of business culture and national culture on written Business English: three early studies

Several early studies, published around the end of the twentieth century, that take a genre approach look at the forms of communication that were used in the business world at that time. Fax communication was a very common form of business communication, as exemplified by the work of Didar Akar and Leena Louhiala-Salminen, both separately and together (e.g. Akar; 2002; Louhiala-Salminen, 1997; Akar & Louhiala-Salminen, 1999), and email correspondence was just beginning to emerge, as discussed by Catherine Nickerson and Jonathan Gains (e.g. Gains, 1999; Nickerson, 1999). These studies investigated how the two business genres had evolved by looking at the form and structure of each one. They also looked at the influence of national and organizational culture on written Business English, together with the similarities that exist in written business genres across the international business community.

Gains (1999), was the first to use an English for Specific Purposes approach to look at the genre of business emails written in English. At that time, as Gains points out in his introduction, there were virtually no textbook materials available for students who needed to write effective emails, with the exception of the 1995 publication by Swales and Feak on academic genres (Swales & Feak, 1995). In his study he compared a corpus of real email examples that had been written by business and academic writers. As noted earlier in this volume, a corpus is a collection of similar examples, usually of written texts, that allows a researcher to compare those texts and then say something useful about the similarities and differences between them. The aim of a corpus analysis is usually to identify the characteristics of a typical example of a specific type of text. A set of emails originating from different sources could form a corpus, for instance, but in Business English research a set of emails and a set of reports most probably would not, because there would be too many differences between them for an analyst to usefully compare them. Gains' work is typical of Business English research using an English for Specific Purposes approach because it refers to real data written by writers in professional settings. As we discussed in Chapter 1, this has been one of the hallmarks of Business English research where the aim has been to understand how a particular business genre is created by the writers that use it. In the next chapter, Chapter 7, we look at other work that has used a combination of real data and simulated or experimental data to find out more about how people interpret a business text written in English.

Gains' data consisted of 116 emails collected at random from the employees of a large British insurance company and several UK universities. Sixty-two of the emails were from the corporate world and the remaining 54 from academia. A total of 59 different writers were represented in the corpus. Gains found that most of the business emails were either used to send information (i.e. were informative) or make requests. Interestingly, he found very few responses to requests, which he suggests may have been because responses to email requests required the use of a different medium, such as telephoning, at the organiza- tion where his data originated. It is possible that as email was a very new medium in the late 1990s, organizations were still developing protocols as to how to incorporate it appropriately into their communication systems. Gains also found that emails were used to issue directives, which provides an early example of email being used to implement management policies.

The communicative purposes of the business emails were distinct from the academic emails in Gains' study in that although the academic writers did use them to send out information, they used them to *respond* to requests rather than to initiate them, and they did not send directives. This is an important finding, as it suggests that different genres with different communicative purposes may evolve within the same medium because the professional community that uses them needs to do different things to accomplish their work. Once he had established why the emails were being used in business settings, Gains then went on to look at the text features by looking at details such as the subject headings, the openings and closings, the level of formality that was used in the emails, and their structure. Some of the findings included the tendency to omit any opening at all (which may have evolved as the norm at the corporation Gains' investigated), the tendency to use formal standard written Business English characterized by full sentences and no word omission, and no evidence of any conversational features (although this was already the case in academic emails in 1999). As we will see in Chapter 8, later studies of email commu- nication have revealed much more divergence from the standard English that was characteristic of business letters in 1999, and much more evidence of conversational features and cross-references both to other business texts and speech events. One final characteristic that Gains found in his data was that the email senders often included the topic of their message in both the subject header and the opening line, or move, in the message. As we will see later in this chapter, the immediate identification of the topic in the message is a characteristic of Anglo-Saxon business writing, and may not be shared across the global business world.

In a second study of corporate email published in the same year, Nickerson (1999) looked at how email in English was used by Dutch and British managers working at a large multinational corporation with offices in the Netherlands. The managers at the multinational provided her with a set of around 900 email messages, out of which she selected a corpus of 200 messages that were all examples of one particular genre; an internal email message where the communicative purpose of the message was the writer's intention to facilitate corporate business by persuading the receiver of the message to carry out a specific action. In the analysis, 100 messages were written by British writers and 100 by Dutch writers. Nickerson first investigated the move structure in the messages, and then looked at whether there were similarities and/or differences in the ways in which the British and Dutch writers incorporated and then realized that move structure. She found that there was no variation in the structure of the messages produced by the two sets of writers. Both sets included two or more of a set of four possible moves (identify the subject of the message; exchange information; justify the action needed; identify the action needed), with the first move an obligatory move that was always included. However, she found that the way in which the moves were realized did vary in some ways between the different national cultures. Corporate culture was responsible for some of the lexis, for instance, in that all the writers used selective Dutch vocabulary that had specific meaning within the multinational – e.g. *ruimte* to refer to a physical location on site at the multinational – in their English messages, and national culture did influence the ways in which some of the moves were realized. For example, the Dutch writers used *we* more often than the British writers, who tended to use *I*, the Dutch writers used words like *very* and *of course* much more often than the British writers, and the British writers used *if* clauses (e.g. *If this is OK, it would be good for you, Jan and I to meet ...*), much more often than the Dutch. The analysis showed that it is possible to identify different language items that could then be a focus in a language course aiming to improve the communication between writers originating from different national cultures.

The studies of fax communication by Didar Akar and Leena Louhiala-Salminen (1999) also revealed differences in the way in which faxes were realized depending on the origin of the writers, and similarities in the genres they identified that were sent by fax across both business cultures. In the 1999 study they completed together, they looked at around 70 Finnish faxes and 90 Turkish faxes, almost all of which were written in English. They found that the data fitted into seven different categories corresponding to seven different communicative purposes: request, inform, confirm, complain, first contact, for your information, and order, and that these were realized by a set of 17 different moves, including some moves like a closing phrase and a signature that were present in all the faxes, and other moves like establishing credentials that only occurred in complaints and first contacts, or providing a reference to previous communication, which always occurred when the purpose of the fax was to inform, confirm, complain, or order. The study also revealed the highly contextualized intertextual nature of fax communication, which means that there were many references to other texts such as emails or reports, or to other organizational events such as meetings. (We will look at intertextuality in more detail in Chapter 9.) It also showed the importance of the business relationships that had been established prior to the communication between the parties involved, where everyone taking part in the fax interaction knew that they all had a shared understanding of the meaning of the fax. If the business relationship had been new, or had not been as well established, then the fax correspondence would have been written in a different way, in that it would have had to include much more explanation. In a precursor to email communication, faxes exhibited some of the hallmarks of an ongoing conversation between the participants that occurred on paper rather than on the phone or in a meeting.

Finally, in other work on faxes, Akar (2002) showed that the order of moves that occurred in fax communication in English in Turkey was very much influenced by the type of organization within which it originated, such that more traditional corporations retained a move structure more typical of traditional Turkish business correspondence. For example, the reason for writing the fax was placed at a late stage in the text, whereas newer more modern organizations in Turkey had developed a style of writing that was much more similar to that used by Finnish business corporations in Louhiala-Salminen's (1997) study, where the reason for writing the fax was placed in initial position in the communication, immediately after the salutation.

These pioneering studies started to reveal some of the important characteristics of Business English genres as they are used across the global business community, including a shared understanding of purpose in some business texts and a shared structure that underpins these texts realized in a set of recognizable moves. On the other hand, they also showed the distinctive influence of business culture in general, national business culture, individual organizational culture, and the languages other than English that many of the writers spoke. They also highlighted the intertextual and highly contextual nature of much written Business English, which depends on the relationships between the writers and readers, and their organizations, in order to successfully interpret the meaning of the texts. We discuss this in more detail in Chapter 9.

In the next section of this chapter, we look at the work of two researchers who have drawn on Bhatia's ideas on genre and related them directly to teaching. The first is the Indianapolis Business Learner Corpus research initiative, overseen by Ulla Connor, and the second is the series of textbooks published by Almut Koester from 2004 onwards, which use a genre approach and the analysis of authentic texts in a data-driven approach to the analysis and teaching of Business English. (For a discussion of Koester's work on spoken genres, see Chapter 5.)

Using a genre approach in the teaching of Business English

The Indianapolis Business Learner Corpus research initiative was a collaborative research project which took place in the 1990s between four academic institutions located in the US, Belgium, and Finland. It is described in detail in the study by Connor et al. (1995). The project focused on the application letter as a business genre that was used across different national cultures, and it referred to Bhatia's work on the structure of application letters as an example of a promotional genre. Unlike the studies that we looked at in the last section, this project relied on a corpus of simulated rather than authentic data in order to identify the differences (and similarities) in the texts produced by university students in the US and Belgium. As we discussed in Part II of this volume in relation to Dow's and Planken's work on negotiations (Dow, 1999; Planken, 2005), it may sometimes be more useful to work with simulated data to investigate what learners do, particularly if the intention is to compare them to experienced professionals.

The Indianapolis Business Learner Corpus was compiled by presenting university students in the US and Belgium with a simulated job advertisement for a summer internship that had been created by the research team. This resulted in a corpus of about 200 letters, all of them written in English. The team randomly selected 74 application letters, 37 written by the students in the US and 37 by the students in Belgium. These letters were then compared in terms of their correctness and clarity with regard to, for instance, the mechanics of the texts (e.g. correct punctuation and spelling), the words (e.g. correct vocabulary), the writer's understanding of the communicative purpose of the text, and the way in which they organized the text. This comparison allowed the researchers to identify a number of different crosscultural variations, including the fact that the US students wrote more and (unsurprisingly, since they were writing in their first language) made fewer mistakes than the Belgian writers. The nature of those mistakes was interesting, however, in that the Belgian students made fewer mistakes in grammar than they did in word choice and spelling, whereas when the US writers made mistakes, they generally did so in grammar. This therefore identified an area of interest for both sets of students that could underpin a teaching or training course on Business English in the future. It is a good example of how a comparative study of this kind can lead directly to an appropriate teaching focus for a specific group of students.

The research team identified six moves that were common to both the US data and the Belgian data: 1) identify the source of the information, 2) apply for the position, 3) provide supporting arguments for the job application, 4) indicate desire for an interview, 5) specify means for further communication, and 6) express politeness or appreciation (Connor et al., 1995, p. 464). When they looked at the realization of these moves, however, they found that only the first and fourth moves were similar in length. In the other four moves, the US students wrote much more than the Belgian students, and in the third move in particular, there was also a difference in content: the Belgian students wrote briefly and in an informative way when they provided supporting arguments for the application, whereas the US students wrote at length in promoting themselves as a candidate and also provided information as to how their candidature would be of benefit to the organization they were applying to. Again, the study clearly identifies similarities and differences that could be referred to as the basis for part of a course in Business English. The similarity in move structure points to a genre that is globally recognizable for the business community, but the differences in the way in which the moves were realized, especially when the candidate provided supporting arguments in the third move, suggest that this could be a focus in a session on cultural differences and how to deal with them, not only for non-native speakers of English, but also for native speakers who need to operate successfully in a multicultural setting. It would be a useful exercise, for instance, for both native and non-native students to consider how they would react to the different versions of the third move – i.e. an informational version of the move compared with a promotional version of the move – and how this would influence their view of the candidate and their chances of being offered an interview. Interestingly, in a follow up study that describes a semester-long interactive course in international writing between students in the US, Belgium, and Finland, the researchers report that the students' application letters had become much more similar, both in length and in the arguments presented to support the application (Connor et al., 1997). The authors attribute this to the discussion on cultural expectations that took place during the course, and the students' resulting awareness that they needed to adjust their writing in order to accommodate these.

Task 6.2 Analyzing different genres

Look back at some of your most recent emails. How would you describe them?

Can you identify different communicative purposes that would allow you to group some of your emails together?

Can you say anything about the structure of the emails that have a shared communicative purpose?

Are the emails conversational or formal? How do you know this?

If you were going to teach a lesson on business emails in English, what would you include and why?

Over the past decade, the UK-based German scholar Almut Koester has authored (and co-authored) a series of textbooks that have incorporated a genre approach to the analysis of authentic Business English texts. As we discussed in Part II of this volume, on spoken Business English, Koester's 2004 publication *The language of work* includes the analysis of meetings and negotiations as prominent examples of spoken interactions, and for written Business English, she focuses on commonly used genres such as promotional letters and emails. Koester's approach is similar to that of Connor and her colleagues in the teaching project based on the US–Belgium application letters data, in that it aims to raise students' awareness of what is happening in a written business text beyond just the mechanics of spelling and grammar. In Koester's approach to promotional letters, for instance, she first presents students with Bhatia's discussion of the structure of sales letters and asks them to re-apply this to a new text. Users of the textbook analyze a UK printer's letter referring to Bhatia's original discussion, and they then continue with a similar letter from the US. Koester provides commentaries on each of these activities and points out both similarities and crosscultural differences between the two Anglo-Saxon cultures in this analysis, as well as the differences that Bhatia identified between South-east Asian and Western business cultures in his work, e.g. the tendency to offer incentives as the third move in the letter that is typical of Singapore and other South-east Asian countries, but which might not be considered appropriate elsewhere. Her work is a very good example of how the findings of a research investigation can be incorporated into a classroom setting for use with students at different levels of language proficiency.

In later publications, Koester has gone on to provide more information on how different analytical approaches can be usefully combined in researching spoken and written communication (2006) and also on effective ways of teaching that communication (2012). She has also most recently co-authored a second textbook for learners of Business English at intermediate level, in which many of her ideas are applied to the creation of the teaching materials (Koester et al., 2012). We look in more detail at her latest work in Part V of this volume (see Chapter 12) when we look at teaching materials and meeting the needs of learners at advanced or near-native levels of proficiency.

Summary

Paltridge (2013) provides an extensive overview of how the genre approach has influenced English for Specific Purposes. As he points out, while a genre approach has frequently been used in understanding more about the written texts and spoken forms of communication that are common in English for academic purposes, it has also been applied to a variety of different genres in Business English, including corporate websites, emails in multinational corporations, sales letters, business faxes, and annual general reports. In this chapter we have traced the development of the English for Specific Purposes approach to the analysis of written Business English texts. We have discussed the pioneering work of Vijay Bhatia and shown how this influenced the work of a number of researchers with an interest in Business English, and we have also looked at the way in which national culture and organizational culture may influence both the form and content of a business text. In the second part of the chapter we looked at how research findings can be incorporated into the classroom and into textbook materials to raise student awareness of how business texts work in different parts of the world. We continue this discussion in the next chapter when we look in particular at how people interpret different types of business texts, and what this means for the Business English classroom.

Chapter 7

Understanding Written Business English

Introduction

In the previous chapter, we introduced the research that has been done on written forms of Business English, including the main approaches that have been applied to the investigation of business documents and the ways in which this research has influenced how people are taught to write. This chapter will shift the focus from product to process, or from the investigation of what characterizes a typical example of a particular type of Business English text to the contexts surrounding how the texts are produced, and how they are interpreted by the people that use them. It will look at the work that has been done on how people create texts and on how people from non-English speaking parts of the world, in particular, interpret English texts. Our focus in this chapter will therefore be on the processes involved in creating business texts, together with the response of readers to common forms of promotional Business English texts such as advertising texts and annual reports. It will also include a discussion on the implications that the findings of both of these types of studies have for Business English teaching.

As discussed in Part II (Chapter 4) when we looked at intercultural business interactions, research focusing on the different strategies people use in spoken Business English is a relatively new addition to the field of English for Specific Purposes. The same is true for studies that have looked at how texts are created and at the response of readers to written forms of Business English. In this chapter we will talk about research within the field of document design in general, with the latter's focus on collaborative writing and reader response, and we will show how this has started to influence the field of English for Specific Purposes with particular reference to the use of English outside Anglo-Saxon business contexts, where Business English as a Lingua Franca is often used. We will draw on the work of those researchers who have pioneered this approach within English for Specific Purposes, including the work of some scholars who have focused on context and collaborative writing processes, and the work of others who have investigated reader response. In each case, we will discuss how studies of context and of reader response to written Business English have been (and could be) incorporated into approaches to teaching.

The field of document design developed from the 1980s onwards and its aim is to understand the processes surrounding the creation of texts and the response of readers to those texts in order to improve the quality of written business documents through their revision. Like English for Specific Purposes it is data-driven rather than theory-driven, and perhaps because of this, several researchers (e.g. Vijay Bhatia, John Flowerdew, Frank van Meurs, Catherine Nickerson, Brigitte Planken) have been active in both fields. Many early studies in document design focused on government documentation providing information to the general public on subjects such as passport renewal in the Netherlands and AIDS awareness in South Africa, but more recent studies have looked at the processes surrounding how people create written Business English texts and then how users respond to them, in particular in situations where both the creators and users of those texts could be non-native speakers. As a result, English for Specific Purposes, with particular reference to business texts, has been enriched in recent years by the insights provided by researchers interested in the processes surrounding the ways in which texts are created, as well as through research studies that have focused on how readers respond to different aspects of the texts. In the sections that follow, we first look at two Hong Kong studies that investigate the creation of documents within the context of accounting together with a teaching project in Hong Kong that used a similar approach to create a set of training materials for business executives. We then focus on three other studies that report on how readers responded to several different promotional genres that include Business English, and on an account of the way in which this approach was used to raise business students' awareness of how Business English as a Lingua Franca can be effectively combined with other languages in advertising texts, while at the same time developing their language skills.

The creation of texts

Flowerdew and Wan (2006) and Flowerdew and Wan (2010) are studies of the creation of a computation tax letter and an audit report respectively, within the accounting and audit community in Hong Kong. The studies investigated how writers worked collaboratively to revise and edit documents. Flowerdew and Wan's (2006) study involved both observation and interviews with a group of tax accountants to investigate how tax computation letters were created; i.e. they looked at the creation of the cover letter that explained to clients how their tax had been prepared by the firm. This meant that in addition to a genre analysis of the texts, which was the same approach as the type of work we described in Chapter 6 where the researcher investigates finished texts, the researchers also carried out what is referred to as an ethnographic analysis; i.e. an analysis designed to understand an activity that takes place within a particular culture from the perspective of the people who carry out that activity. Its aim was to provide a thick description of an activity as it is understood by the people involved in that activity in a given context (see also Chapter 6). In Flowerdew and Wan's study, this involved uncovering how tax accountants collaborated in order to structure and write the texts that they needed to complete their business activities, in addition to understanding the role that was then played by the texts themselves. This is why the researchers needed to observe the tax accountants and interview them: so that the accountants could explain' to the researchers what they were doing and why. The interviewees described a process which involved a combination of the creation of new text and the recycling of existing text, together with a certain amount of collaborative work where colleagues read each other's drafts for content accuracy and accuracy in English, together with an additional review from the manager.

All the accountants participating in the study were non-native speakers of English, mostly Cantonese. While their discussions often took place in Cantonese, the tax letters were generated in English. Interestingly, several of the tax accountants who were interviewed commented on the fact that they had never been taught to write tax computation letters despite the fact that they are an important written business genre that they regularly need to write in English. The study implies that although students may certainly find it useful to look at finished examples of the genres that they will need to reproduce in English in order to get their work done, it is also important that they understand the processes surrounding how such genres are produced and the skills that they need to develop to facilitate such processes. The tax accountants in the Flowerdew and Wan study, for instance, needed to know how to collaborate to co-create a text, and it was also necessary for them to be able to discuss that text in their own language while creating it in English. Later in this section, we will discuss an account of how a group of researchers took the development of these additional skills into consideration in the design of a Business English training course.

In the second study, Flowerdew and Wan (2010) look at another Business English genre created by auditors in Hong Kong: the audit report. Again, in addition to the type of analysis that we described in Chapter 6, the researchers used an ethnographic approach involving observation and interviews in addition to the analysis of existing texts, with the specific aim of generating information that would be of use in teaching. The researchers observed the creation of the audit report from start to finish, including the audit assignment which preceded it and the drafting of the report, and they also conducted follow-up interviews with the audit team and their manager. Again, as we will discuss in more detail in Chapter 9, the creation of the audit report was characterized by intertextuality (i.e. cross-referencing to other written documents and spoken interactions), and to interdiscursivity (i.e. cross-referencing between written documents, spoken interactions, the application of professional conventions and the achievement of corporate goals). The observation period also allowed the researchers to identify a number of different processes and different types of information that the participants needed to carry out or use effectively in order to complete the audit. These included, for instance, the ability to carry out a number of complicated speaking tasks such as explaining, asking for information, and problem-solving (completed in either Cantonese or Mandarin), the ability to combine existing templates and additional original writing in English in the audit report, and the ability to recognize and use a large number of technical terms in English that were required in interactions that otherwise took place in Cantonese and Mandarin.

As Flowerdew and Wan (2010) observe, the combination of a linguistic analysis using a genre approach and a contextual analysis using an ethnographic approach allowed them to identify a number of different competencies that the tax accountants and auditors they investigated needed to acquire in order to effectively complete the task of writing the tax computation letter and audit report. These included complicated speaking tasks in one or more different languages, an extensive knowledge of technical terms in English, and the ability to combine existing material (in English) with new material. The studies show how different types of information can be collected using a variety of research methods, which can then be used as the basis for a training or teaching course in the relevant form of Business English. Rather than simply considering the form and content of a particular text in Business English, studies like these underline the importance of also understanding how a text is created and then finding ways to help students to develop the skills they need to participate effectively in creating that text.

The study that follows is an account of how a research team incorporated both genre and collaborative processes into the design of a writing course for business executives.

Task 7.1 Carrying out an ethnographic survey

Talk to a business person that you know and find out about the types of writing that they do at work and the processes they follow in order to do this. Find out as much as you can about the skills and strategies that your interviewee thinks are necessary to carry out their writing tasks effectively at work, and the skills that they felt they needed to acquire when they first started working. If you are in a non-English speaking country, ask your interviewee about the different languages they use at work.

Prepare a set of interview questions in advance to structure your conversation and make notes as if you are planning a training course designed to help your interviewee improve their business writing skills. Plan your questions as if you are taking an ethnographic approach and try to obtain a thick description of your contact's writing and business activities, including all the different skills they need to carry them out effectively.

Context and collaboration in the teaching of written Business English

Baxter et al. (2002) describe the development of a training course in Business English writing for the Hong Kong Jockey Club. This involved both a detailed analysis of the texts that managers at the Jockey Club needed to write and an analysis of the collaborative and business processes in the context surrounding those texts. It included an extensive needs analysis which led to the identification and analysis of important written genres at the club, and it also referred to the findings of a set of questionnaires and interviews which were designed to find out more about the context in which those genres were produced. The researchers therefore combined three different research approaches to gain a thick description of writing at the Jockey Club: a genre analysis of a specific set of texts, an ethnographic analysis of the processes surrounding the writing of the texts, and a needs analysis to identify which skills should be included in a training course.

The team followed the production of 30 committee papers, which allowed them to carry out the genre analysis at several different points in the drafting process, so that they could see how a committee paper progressed through the organization, and they also interviewed 20 executives in depth, asking them questions such as What types of writing does your job require? How many people are involved in the process of writing committee papers? and What are the hardest parts of writing a committee paper? This needs analysis allowed the research team to identify the committee paper as a genre that was a crucial part of the writing done at the Jockey Club, and also enabled them to differentiate between the tasks carried out by different people within the organization. The investigation revealed that the Jockey Club executives needed training in how to write collaboratively and strategically and that it was their insufficient skills in these two areas that were causing most difficulties rather than the more obvious difficulties associated with writing Business English documents (such as grammar and style). An appropriate training course therefore needed to combine all of these elements.

Baxter et al. (2002) describe how they translated the findings of their genre and ethnographic investigation into a set of training materials. This included materials on how individual writers could improve their own skills in writing a committee paper, but it also considered effective ways of facilitating the process of writing, such as how to gather the information necessary to start the process, how to draft a paper strategically, and how to manage other people while they were engaged in the process of drafting and writing. The research team created a two-day training course for the Jockey Club executives involving case studies followed by group case analyses, team presentations, and considerable reference to authentic examples of committee papers at various stages of preparation in the drafting process and not just the completed product. The participants were also presented with ways of structuring their writing effectively, such as Blicq and Moretto's Summary-Background-Facts-Outcome model (1998), which they used to analyze existing committee papers and then reconstruct them. The Jockey Club project used an English for Specific Purposes approach, drawing on a combination of ethnography, genre analysis, and needs analysis in order to analyze and contextualize the target documents and develop some of the training materials. It then also drew on the team's knowledge of the business and management processes that existed at the Jockey Club at that time to decide how to approach those materials once the course was underway. As in Lockwood's account of the development of an appropriate training course in the call centre industry that we profiled in Chapter 1 (Lockwood, 2012), it was only possible to do this by understanding not just the Business English interaction or document, but also the processes that created it and the business processes that it facilitated – i.e. understanding the business event that the interaction or document represented.

As we discuss in Part IV of this book when we talk in more detail about the modern business world, Business English practitioners often need to be prepared to go beyond the boundaries of a single written text or spoken interaction and understand more about both the immediate context surrounding that individual communication and the wider business context within which it is used.

In the next section, we consider a number of studies that combine an English for Specific Purposes approach with an experimental investigation of reader response. We conclude the chapter with an account of a similar study which was partly carried out by business students in order to increase their awareness of how advertising in English impacts the global business world.

The response to texts

Planken et al. (2010), Hornikx et al. (2010), and de Groot et al. (2011) all look at the response of readers to the use of Business English as a Lingua Franca in different types of promotional texts. Planken et al. (2010) investigate the use of English in Polish product advertisements, Hornikx et al. (2010) the use of English slogans in the Netherlands, and de Groot et al. (2011) the response of financial analysts to annual general reports in English originating in the Netherlands and the UK.

Planken et al. (2010) investigate the effects of using English advertising in Polish glossy magazines targeted at young, educated Polish women. A set of respondents – young, educated women representing the target group for the glossy magazines – were presented with different versions of six product advertisements. These were either the original English versions of the texts that had appeared in the magazine, or the same advertisements translated into Polish. The respondents were asked about their perceptions of the brand or product shown in the advertisement, their attitude towards the advertisement, and whether they would purchase the product. They were also asked about whether they could understand the text: e.g. could they understand the

English phrase *You look great*. If they said that they were able to understand the text, then they were asked to give either a translation or a paraphrase of the English text.

There were no statistically significant differences between the English or Polish versions of the advertisements in terms of how the texts were perceived, how the respondents felt about the brand or product, or whether they would consider buying the product, and there were only a few differences in comprehension. In general, advertisements written in English did not create any comprehension problems – but equally, people did not view advertisements written in English any more favourably than advertisements written in Polish. The study therefore found that the use of Business English as a Lingua Franca did not lead to a more positive association with the product or brand, as some advertising agencies claim is the case; nor did it make it more likely that a consumer would purchase a product if it was advertised in English. On the other hand, however, the young, highly educated respondents who participated in the study did not appear to have any difficulty in understanding the English version of the texts. The researchers observe that "English is now so widespread in advertising in EFL countries – that it is no longer regarded or perceived as 'special'" (2010, p. 239). Empirical research like this provides useful insights into how written Business English is perceived in advertising texts and, as the authors suggest, similar projects can also be used with Business English students at advanced levels of language proficiency to raise their awareness of the effects of using English in international advertising.

Hornikx et al. (2010) look in more detail at the effectiveness of using English as a Lingua Franca in written business texts. They detail an experiment in which Dutch respondents were presented with car advertisements with authentic English slogans and were then asked to express a preference for either the English slogan or its Dutch equivalent. The English slogans had been rated before the experiment by another group of Dutch respondents as being either easy to understand (e.g. "Driving is believing") or difficult to understand (e.g. "Once driven, forever smitten"). A hundred and twenty people were asked to rate the advertisements in terms of their appreciation of the English slogans, their preference for the same slogan in either English or Dutch, and whether or not they could understand and then translate or paraphrase the slogan. The findings showed that the respondents had much more difficulty paraphrasing the slogans that had been rated as difficult than paraphrasing the easy slogans, and they also appreciated the easy English slogans more than the difficult English slogans. In addition, in advertisements where the slogan was easy to understand, they generally preferred the English version of the advertisement to the Dutch version; but if the slogan was difficult to understand, they had no preference for either the Dutch version or the English version. The researchers conclude that "the difficulty of the English slogan more clearly affected people's preference for English or the local, Dutch language. English was preferred to Dutch when it was easy to understand; when it was difficult to understand, English was appreciated as much as the Dutch equivalent" (2010, p. 184). As they observe, although English was viewed positively by the majority of their respondents and it appeared to have an added value if it was included in the advertisements (as long as it was easy to understand), it also seemed clear that whether a person can comprehend an advertisement affects how much they appreciate it. The study lends support to the standardization of global advertising using written Business English, as its use was viewed as either positive or neutral by all of the respondents. As in the previous study on Polish magazine advertisements, empirical research like this can be replicated with student groups at more advanced levels to raise their awareness of how language choices can be used to both positive and negative effect in promotional texts. Non-native speakers could work with the English slogans used in their own country, for instance, and investigate how easy these are to understand. They could then look at whether people appreciate the English slogans or their equivalents in the language used in the local context, and how this affects their response to an advertising text.

Finally in this section, the study by de Groot et al. (2011) looks at the response of financial analysts to the texts and photographs taken from Dutch-English and British-English annual reports. The 2011 study builds on an earlier genre study (de Groot et al., 2006) that had established that there are both textual and pictorial differences between Dutch-English and British-English managerial forewords in annual general reports as a result of differences in the respective business contexts such as different historical business conventions. The 2011 study then used these differences and investigated the effectiveness of texts and photos that are characteristic of Dutch-English and British-English management statements, by running an experiment with a representative target audience: a group of financial analysts based in the UK. The research team created two management statements with either Dutch-English or British-English features, and 35 analysts based in London were asked a number of questions about each of the corporations represented in the statements, including what they thought about the corporation's reputation, whether they would be willing to invest in the corporation, what their attitude to the text was, how comprehensible they thought the text was, and which of the two texts they preferred. Overall, the study showed that the UK-based analysts preferred the British-English version of the text to the Dutch-English version. They also preferred specific details in the texts that were typical of British-English management statements, including specific types of content information (e.g. in the descriptions of board details, corporate social responsibility, and dividends), the structuring of the information in the text (e.g. with headings), and the style of photographs that were included (e.g. pictures of managers looking away from the camera, which occur in British-English reports but are rare in Dutch-English reports). In general, respondents reported that although their preference for a different version of the text would not affect their willingness to invest in the corporation, it did affect how positive they considered a corporation's image to be. Unlike the previous study we looked at in this section on car advertising slogans, therefore, this study suggests that annual reports should be adapted for different global audiences if corporations want to be successful with different groups of stakeholders. The study is interesting because it shows that there may be consequences when corporations decide to communicate using Business English as a Lingua Franca. The work is also unusual in that it combines text and pictures, both in the 2006 genre study and in the 2011 response study. Students at higher levels of language proficiency could easily work with texts like annual reports to look at crosscultural differences that continue to exist even if a business organization opts for Business English in their corporate documentation. Annual reports are easily accessible on corporate websites and can provide practitioners with a rich source of information to use with advanced Business English classes. Students could be asked to identify differences between annual reports originating in different business cultures, for example, and then investigate what effect these differences could have on a particular target audience.

In the next and final section, we look at a project, partly carried out by students, that incorporated both the analysis of text and reader response in an investigation of how Business English is used and perceived in advertising texts.

Task 7.2 Using text analysis in the classroom

Look at the advertisements in a magazine from a non-English speaking country and select any that include English words. List the slogans that are either partly or completely in English. Try to rank these slogans according to how easy or difficult they are and provide a paraphrase for each one, either in English or in the magazine's main language.

Design a lesson for students of Business English at different levels of proficiency in which you use the advertising materials and slogans that you found.

Using reader response in the teaching of written Business English

Nickerson et al. (2005) is a discussion of a large project that looks at the use of Business English in a number of different types of promotional texts (e.g. corporate websites, print advertising, and TV commercials) in several countries in the European Union (Belgium, the Netherlands, France, Germany, and Spain). The project was carried out by 160 senior business students who worked with a group of multilingual, multicultural faculty members to investigate how much English is used in print advertising in glossy magazines in each of the target countries, including where it was used, and what effect it had on consumers. As in the study by Planken et al. (2010) on Polish advertising, the intention was to investigate whether a standardized global advertising policy using only English as a Lingua Franca was more or less likely to be successful than a localized approach taking the respective local languages into account. As the authors suggest, investigating the possible mismatch between advertising policies and consumer response to those policies not only contributes to our further understanding of how written Business English operates in promotional texts, but also provides "a useful way of raising student awareness of the use of English in business contexts and the effects this may have on the intended target audiences" (Nickerson, et al., 2005, p. 335). The project was designed to be accessible to business students without a specialized background in applied linguistics, and although it assumed an intermediate level of English language proficiency, many of the students involved spoke it as their third language. To start the project, the faculty research team put together a set of promotional genres for each of the target countries and the students were asked to decide how much and what type of English was used in each one. For instance, some groups looked at print advertising, some at TV advertising, and some at corporate websites. As in the studies that we discussed in Chapter 6, this phase of the project took a genre approach and focused on the text features in the texts, specifically the use of English lexis. Students used current Dutch, French, German, and Spanish dictionaries to check if specific words that seemed to be English had in fact been accepted in these target languages (for example the word *manager* is now an acceptable Dutch word), and they also checked whether English words that were not in their target language dictionary were being used with the same meaning as they were either in an English dictionary or on a UK website (using a Google search to investigate this). Finally, they also noted any complete phrases in English that had been used in their genres (e.g. "Your last stop before the top" (p. 337)). At this stage in the project, the students showed an increasing awareness of the impact that English has as a lingua franca and an international business language, and they also collaborated with other student groups working with one of the other European languages to see if there were similarities or differences between the data the students had collected. In other words, they had effectively moved beyond their usual role as language learners and had started to think about how Business English works in practice. As we discussed in Chapter 2, English is now in widespread use around the world to varying degrees in different types of business texts, and this part of the project could be easily adapted for use in other (non-European) contexts, and for students at different levels of English language proficiency.

Once the students had completed their genre analysis, they set up a study to investigate the response of an audience to the use of Business English in a similar way to the Polish study of advertising in glossy magazines and the study of English slogans in Dutch car advertising discussed earlier in this chapter. Nickerson et al. (2005) describe a comparable set of student projects that all looked at advertising in glossy magazines and subsequently used a questionnaire and a set of authentic and manipulated advertisement texts in English and their equivalents in Dutch, French, German, and Spanish to investigate the audience's reaction to advertising in English versus local languages. Again, in this part of the project, the need to generate equivalent texts in various languages to create the experimental materials proved to be highly motivating for the students and prompted a great deal of discussion on how the meaning of a particular word or phrase could best be captured from one language to another. As we discussed earlier in the car slogans' study (Hornikx et al., 2010), it is relatively easy to find different slogans or other parts of an advertisement at differing levels of difficulty for non-native speakers, which means that an exercise involving the creation of equivalent texts can also be adjusted to accommodate different levels of language proficiency. As in the project described by Planken et al. (2010), the questionnaire included questions about attitudes to the different language versions of the advertisement, about the respondents' willingness to buy the product featured in the text, and whether or not they could understand the (English) text fragments. Finally, in the last stage of the project, the student researchers analyzed the data collected through the questionnaire, including the translations or paraphrases given for the target slogans or other text fragments, (e.g. "Smile with all your senses").

Nickerson et al. (2005) discuss a number of ways in which this project was relevant for English for Specific Purposes. First of all, it focused the students' attention on the interaction between English and other local languages in a set of prominent and easily accessible written business texts. Collecting a comparable corpus in order to replicate the project would be relatively simple in most parts of the world and could be used to start a discussion on the role played by Business English in promotional genres. In addition, working with slogans and other text fragments to find equivalent meanings in English and the students' own language can help students to develop their language skills with reference to authentic business texts in addition to raising their awareness of the importance of comprehension in conveying a promotional message. Finally, while genre analysis is crucial in helping students to understand more about the form, content, and communicative purpose of Business English texts, projects like this one also provide students with invaluable insights into how such texts are perceived.

Summary

In this chapter, we have discussed two additional developments in English for Specific Purposes as important ways of understanding how Business English works: the contextualization of texts, investigated through ethnographic research, and the response of users to texts, investigated through experimental research. We have explored these developments and looked at how they have influenced English for Specific Purposes, most especially for those researchers with an interest in business texts, and we have shown how both an ethnographic approach and an experimental approach can be combined with genre analysis to tell us more about how and why Business English documents are written in the way that they are. We have considered several studies that have expanded the analysis of a set of written texts, either by asking people how they were written or by asking people to read them and respond to them, and we have looked at how this information can then be incorporated into Business English teaching materials. In the next chapter, we continue this discussion and focus on several of the most recent studies of written business documents that have explored how research can be used as the basis for teaching.

Chapter 8

Teaching Written Business English

Introduction

In the previous chapter, we looked at how an understanding of context and an understanding of how people respond to texts have both been influential in recent English for Specific Purposes work with a focus on written Business English. In this chapter, we will continue that discussion and will focus on the work of three researchers who have investigated either context or how people respond to texts and have then used this information to provide commentaries on the best ways in which to teach Business English. Evans (2012) focuses on business email and uses the findings of an extensive study within the Hong Kong service sector to provide suggestions as to how to teach it, Gimenez (2014) builds partly on his previous work on business emails and computer mediated communication (see Gimenez, 2000; 2009) to investigate the role that technology can play in classroom activities, and finally, Zhang (2013) draws on a study of the response of business professionals to business texts written by students and discusses the implications of these findings for teaching. Significantly, all three are active researchers who take an English for Specific Purposes approach in their investigation of business genres, including an investigation of both the texts and their context, and all three are also experienced teachers of Business English.

The influence of context and the Business English classroom

In this section, we look at the work of Stephen Evans and Julio Gimenez, who have both considered how the real-life business context operates and the ways in which their insights can be incorporated into the Business English classroom. Their work comprises some of the very few studies that have been done on email and computer-mediated communication since Gains' (1999) study, which we highlighted in Chapter 6.

Evans' (2012) study provides numerous insights into how to teach business email in the Business English classroom. As he points out, although email permeates all forms of business life it is often absent from business textbooks and has failed to receive much research attention in English for Specific Purposes. Evans presents email as a telling example of the fact that there is often little correlation between what happens in the business context and what is presented to students in published materials. While there is increasing evidence, both empirical and anecdotal, that email is a mainstay of how business people carry out their work, this is rarely discussed or practised in teaching contexts. Evans' aim is to bridge this gap by providing English for Specific Purposes practitioners with a number of suggestions – based on his investigation of business email – that can be incorporated into the Business English classroom.

In a previous study, published in 2010, Evans describes an extensive investigation of the use of English in professional communication across four key service industries in Hong Kong, which also forms the background for the 2012 discussion (Evans, 2010). As part of the wider study, a paper-based questionnaire was distributed to 4,148 professionals together with an online version sent out to just under 30,000 others, representing a wide range of academic disciplines and business activities including accounting, insurance, law, logistics, financial services, and tourism. Two thousand and thirty questionnaires were returned, which allowed Evans to build a picture of how different languages were used in business at the time the questionnaire was distributed (in 2008) as well as identify the key genres that were being used to facilitate business. The findings of the questionnaire survey showed that English was considered to be the most important language respondents used for written communication in their professional lives, alongside Cantonese, which was the most important language for spoken communication. As discussed in the previous chapter, Flowerdew and Wan (2006; 2010) also found that English dominated in writing, while Cantonese dominated in speaking. Evans (2010) observes that meetings and discussions often take place in Cantonese, but are reported in English, and equally that presentations may also be conducted in Cantonese; but he refers to other written documentation, like reports and proposals, that are generally written in English. These findings suggest that English for Specific Purposes practitioners need to recreate situations that simulate the language context surrounding the production of written Business English, including discussions in the local language (or languages) rather than in English, if that tends to be the norm. As we discussed in Chapter 2, the use of Business English as a Lingua Franca is now commonplace in global business, and it seems likely that many business people complete some work tasks in their own language and others in English. Hill and van Zyl (2002) observe a similar situation in South Africa, where English is often used for written documents alongside Afrikaans and other African languages in spoken interactions. Nickerson (2000) describes the use of spoken Dutch in an Anglo-Dutch multinational corporation together with the requirement to use English in official documentation, and Gimenez (2002) reports on the same situation at the Argentinian subsidiary of a Swiss multinational corporation, where Spanish and English co-existed (sometimes uneasily) side by side.

In all these cases, empirical research revealed that written documents were generally produced in English, but that the spoken interactions that facilitated them often took place in another language.

Evans (2010) identifies seven different written genres that were produced in Business English in Hong Kong. These were external email messages, internal email messages, reports, letters, memos, faxes, and minutes. All of these were written at least once or twice a month, and both types of email message (external and internal) were written by most of the participants at least once or twice a week. The same set of genres was also identified when the participants were asked about their reading activities in English, alongside several other genres such as websites, newsletters, and promotional materials. Unsurprisingly, internal and external emails were read by all the participants more frequently than any of the other document types. Despite the lack of attention that has been given to business email in published textbooks, these findings are a clear indication that business people in Hong Kong need to be able to read and respond effectively to large amounts of email written in English.

Evans (2012) describes three sets of data that he refers to in making his detailed observations about business email: 1) a set of interviews with Chinese professionals who needed English for their work, 2) a series of case studies lasting for a week at a time, in which four of the professionals recorded their activities in half-hourly segments with reference to a discourse checklist and one of the professionals was shadowed for a day by a member of the research team (who took notes on the communication activities that he/she observed), and 3) the analysis of 50 email chains, which included over 400 email messages. As in the studies by Flowerdew and Wan (2006; 2010) that we looked at in the previous chapter, Evans' study therefore combined an ethnographic approach (based on the data he collected through the case studies and interviews) and a genre approach (based on the text analysis). This allowed him to both describe and contextualize his target communication. As a result of the genre approach, the study reveals the "length, language and structure" of the email messages (2012, p. 202), but at the same time, the ethnographic approach provides contextual information about the role that email plays in internal and external communication, the way in which it interfaces with spoken communication, and the importance of intertextuality in how it is constructed. While a traditional pedagogical approach would have been limited to the findings of the genre analysis and would have dealt with email in isolation from any other communication events, Evans suggests using a simulation-based approach, similar to the approach used by the team at the Hong Kong Jockey Club to train executives to write committee papers that we discussed in Chapter 7. As we show in what follows, a simulation approach recreates the activities that surround business email and involves more than just writing skills.

Evans describes the insights he gained from the interviews, case studies, and the email chain analysis in the 2012 study. In the in-depth interviews, for instance, there were almost 400 comments by the interviewees that referred to email correspondence, whereas there were only around 130 that referred to both meetings and reports. In addition, the case studies confirmed that reading and writing emails (in English) was a major preoccupation for the four professionals who completed the discourse checklists, including the individual who was shadowed in the observation period. Evans identifies six key findings that were related to the ways in which email was used; 1) email and spoken communication are interlinked, 2) internal and external emails are distinct and should be dealt with separately when teaching Business English, 3) business professionals have to deal with large numbers of emails every day, which means that they need to be able to respond quickly and briefly, 4) the structure used in authentic emails often diverges from the models that are presented in textbook materials, 5) the authentic emails were characterized by intertextuality, which again is largely absent in the models presented in textbooks, and 6) the authentic emails, particularly those used for internal communication, were sometimes inaccurate in terms of grammar and informal in terms of style, suggesting that real world communication can be both inaccurate and inappropriate – a situation that is not reflected in textbooks (Evans, 2012). Evans provides a set of pedagogical implications for Business English teachers on the basis of what he found, which can be summarized as follows:

1 Email should be included in any Business English course, as although it is often absent in many textbooks, it is a crucial part of business communication.
2 Although it may prove impossible to recreate the complex nature of the business environment, it is important to incorporate email into classroom activities designed to teach Business English in the same way in which it operates in real life – i.e. not as a discrete item, but in combination with other forms of business communication.
3 Classroom tasks involving email should require reading, writing, listening, and speaking skills, and should be embedded within other important business genres such as meetings, reports, presentations, and proposals. A simulation-based approach could be the best way to achieve this, with clearly defined roles for the participants and the built-in need to collaborate and communicate efficiently and effectively in order to complete the tasks involved.
4 Writing tasks involving email work best if students are involved in creating a chain of communication – as in real-life situations – rather than just constructing the first and second message in the chain.

Evans' observations on how to teach email within the Business English classroom are important because they are based on authentic situations in business and the discussion of empirical findings. They echo the calls made by Kankaanranta and Louhiala-Salminen (2010), discussed in Chapter 2, for the emphasis in teaching Business English (as a Lingua Franca) to be on developing students' professional competence in dealing strategically with different forms of communication, with less emphasis on grammatical and stylistic accuracy. In the final part of this book, we consider several textbooks that have taken the approach that Evans advocates into account in their use of simulations in the classroom.

Since the mid-1990s, Julio Gimenez has been publishing on various aspects of English for Specific Purposes, and much of his work has been related to the use of Business English and computer-mediated communication. In an early study of email, for instance, published in 2000, he compares a corpus of 60 email messages with a corpus of 40 business letters in order to investigate the impact that the relatively informal spoken style used in email was having on other forms of written Business English. The study looks at the mechanical characteristics of business email at that time (e.g. the use of abbreviations and informal forms of address), but it also starts to explore how the medium had begun to impact the business context (e.g. the gradual change in business practice that occurred because, unlike letters, email could be sent at any time and received simultaneously). Gimenez suggests, as a result, that English for Specific Purposes practitioners should incorporate email into their Business English classes, for example by asking students to analyze their own authentic emails. Despite this early acknowledgement that email was, and would increasingly become, an important communication medium for business, as Evans (2012) too has observed, it is still not adequately covered in published textbook materials.

Six years later, Gimenez (2006) returned to email and looked at how it had increased in complexity and significance within modern business. Rather than looking only at isolated examples of emails, as had been the norm for most researchers until that time, this study is one of the first to consider the embedded nature of business email, which means that the receiver of one message must refer to other messages, often in a chain, in order to make sense of what he or she is reading. In addition to completing a genre analysis of a corpus of single email messages and email chains, Gimenez looked at the relationship between the possibilities afforded by email as a medium of communication and the changing demands of international business communication. For instance, the flexibility inherent in email communication (because emails can be sent at any time) provides a way of facilitating the work of global teams who may be operating in different time zones. A single email can be sent to the whole team and involve all of them in the process of decision-making. The analysis of the texts in the 2006 study is one of the first attempts to provide empirical evidence for the interdiscursive and intertextual nature of email: i.e. the fact that emails frequently cross-reference to other forms of communication, including faxes, telephone calls, conference calls, and other web-based materials available on the internet.

Most recently, Gimenez (2014) looks at the role that technology can play in teaching Business English. The study takes an ethnographic approach, similar to that taken in the studies by Flowerdew and Wan discussed in Chapter 7, and focuses on the multi-communication practices that could be observed in four multinational companies in London, representing four different industries: telecommunications, banking, marketing, and management consultancy.

Gimenez defines multi-communication as "holding multiple conversations at the same time" (2014, p. 1), and the study seeks to identify the processes that business people need in order to facilitate effective multi-communication. The data was collected using a survey, a set of interviews, several observational shadowing sessions, and the compilation of a corpus consisting of different business documents. Alongside demographics, the survey collected information on communication practices, tools, and experience, and it also included reference to tasks that are common in the business environment such as emailing, using the telephone, and texting. Fifty people completed the survey and 13 of them were then interviewed in more detail about their responses. Finally, three of the interviewees were shadowed over three days and their multi-communication practices were observed and recorded. The study aimed to investigate the following questions:

1   What are the main skills that are required for multi-communication?
2   What is the relationship between multi-communication and the traditional view of effective communication in the workplace?
3   What is the number of conversations that a person can hold simultaneously?
(Gimenez, 2014, p. 6)

Gimenez identifies four main skills that facilitate effective multi-communication. He refers to these as *thematic threading, presence allocation, audience profiling,* and *media packaging*. Thematic threading means that an individual is skilled in clustering different communication events on the same subject and then multitasking around them (e.g. demonstrating the ability to send an email and simultaneously carry on a telephone conversation on the same topic). Presence allocation means that an individual has sufficient skills in using the media available to them so that they can manage their online presence efficiently and flexibly – for example through the strategic use of instant messaging, which allows a skilled user to participate in several conversations simultaneously. Media packaging involves combining different media at the same time to communicate efficiently (e.g. the simultaneous use of email, instant messaging, and mobile phone). As Gimenez observes, being effective at media packaging means not only developing good individual skills, but also being aware of the media provided by an organization and understanding how to use them efficiently. Finally, audience profiling involves understanding the different audiences that an individual needs to deal with in business and then clustering similar audiences together according to their purposes, needs, or demands in order to save time. The interviewees suggested that skilful audience profiling could lead to more efficiency, although perhaps at the expense of really connecting with the individual audiences.

Gimenez observes that multi-communication "with its emphasis on being able to juggle communication tasks, people and media seems to be changing the way effective communication is being conceptualized in contemporary organizations" (2014, p 9). In the organizations he studied, for instance, there was a shift from individual attention, empathy, and communicative effectiveness towards efficiency and audience profiling. The business people that Gimenez interviewed frequently talked about efficiency, multitasking, and saving time, and the profiling of audiences implied the use of fewer individualized responses and more recycling and reusing of existing materials. We discussed strategies like this in the previous chapter, when Flowerdew and Wan (2010) reported that the auditors they studied needed to be skilled in combining existing templates with additional original writing in English in order to produce an audit report. In addition, in Gimenez's study, most of the respondents preferred to use communication media such as email and instant messaging because this allowed them to multitask rather than requiring their focused attention on one individual task (as would be the case in face-to-face communication). Gimenez reports that the participants in his study were frequently engaged in a number of different communications at any given time; this could involve, for instance, the use of email and instant messaging, drafting a Word document, drafting a presentation, and surfing the Internet. Many reported that they would often work simultaneously on two or three of these activities without this leading to a breakdown in the communication.

Finally, drawing on his findings, Gimenez (2014) provides a set of tasks, based on each of the multi-communication tasks he identified in real life, to be used in the Business English classroom with students at intermediate levels of proficiency and above. For example, in order to develop skills in thematic threading, which requires business people to group communication tasks on a shared topic, students are provided with a set of three email tasks and two telephone tasks, relating to two different topics in a business simulation, which need to be completed as quickly as possible. The students are told that they will need to work on more than one task simultaneously, and before they complete the tasks they are asked to decide how best to group them. The simulation therefore develops their writing and speaking skills in Business English, but also focuses on the development of their communicative strategies in deciding how best to approach the tasks beforehand. Similarly for presence allocation, where business people can decide to control their participation through media such as email and instant messaging, Gimenez provides a business simulation that requires students to solve a technical problem for a customer involving individual students playing the roles of the customer and the customer service representative, and an additional colleague who acts as a troubleshooter. The communication with the customer and the service representative, and between the representative and the additional colleague, all takes place via instant messaging, and the participants are required to communicate effectively in English via the medium while at the same time deciding at which point in the discussion it is appropriate for them to withdraw or continue their participation. To develop skills in media packaging, Gimenez provides a set of four tasks (two email tasks, one instant messaging task, and one telephone task) with the simulation given in Textbox 8.1. The students are required to decide in advance how to organize the different tasks and which ones to complete at the same time. Again, the use of Business English is only a part of completing the simulation effectively, and the various tasks are not completed in isolation (as they would be in a traditional classroom setting), but simultaneously (as they are likely to be carried out in a real-life business setting).

Textbox 8.1 An example of a simulation task

You are on the phone with a colleague at the same time that you are writing a reply to an email you have just received when a customer logs onto the instant messaging service to request information. You don't actually want to stop the telephone conversation with your colleague as he/she will be very helpful in dealing with these tasks simultaneously (Gimenez, 2014, p. 13).

Finally, in order to develop skills in audience profiling, Gimenez (2014) provides the details of three potential customers with different demographics and different requirements. The students are first required to profile them according to a given set of variables, such as how to address them, what communication media to use, whether to use formal or informal language, etc., and the business simulation then requires a student to communicate with all three customers at the same time using telephone, email, and instant messaging, thereby developing their language skills in spoken and written Business English, their skills in dealing with different audiences, and their skills at using the different communication media.

Gimenez's work is very important for English for Specific Purposes in general and for Business English in particular, because it provides both empirical research and concrete examples to support a set of classroom activities on written Business English.

In Part IV, we will continue this discussion and unpack how spoken and written forms of Business English communication intertwine in the modern business world. In the next section, we consider how business people respond to the writing produced by students of Business English and what this means for teaching.

Task 8.1 Developing classroom tasks to teach email communication

Read Gimenez (2014) and look in detail at the multi-communication tasks he provides at the end for use in the Business English classroom. Compare these to the tasks provided for practising email communication in a Business English textbook that you use or with which you are familiar.

What are the most important differences between the two sets of tasks? Which do you think are most effective, and why?

Gimenez, J. (2014). Multi-communication and the business English class: Research meets pedagogy. *English for Specific Purposes, 35,* 1–16.

The response of business practitioners to student texts

Zhang's (2013) study looks at the response of business practitioners to students' texts. As we discussed in Chapter 7, studies of reader response to the various characteristics of business texts or interactions are a relatively recent – and rare – addition to English for Specific Purposes. Studies that have looked at how the Business English produced by students compares to the Business English produced by professionals, and how professionals respond to the spoken and written Business English produced by students, are even more infrequent. The study by Planken (2005) on safe talk in negotiations that we discussed in Part II of this volume is one of the few such studies to look at spoken Business English and the difference between students and experienced professionals, and the 2000 study by Seshadri and Theye (2000) remains an isolated example of the mismatch that occurs when business professionals and academic business professors evaluate the same student-authored reports. As we discussed in Chapter 4, Planken (2005) showed that there were a number of significant differences between the safe talk used in negotiations by professionals and the safe talk used by students, and likewise, Seshadri and Theye (2000) showed that while business professors place more emphasis on the mechanics of writing (e.g. grammar and vocabulary), business professionals are more interested in the content of reports. An interesting unexpected finding in the Seshadri and Theye study, however, was that although business professionals paid relatively little attention to the surface features of the texts, they were as critical as their academic counterparts of what they considered to be violations of business writing style. Given the lack of research that takes the views of business practitioners into account, Zhang's work can be considered as both timely and useful, not only in highlighting how experienced business people respond to students' attempts at business writing, but also in discussing the implications of their observations for teaching.

Zhang's study is extensive in that it draws on more than 1,000 comments made by eight business professionals who looked at 40 different texts written by five Business English students representing a range of different business genres such as application letters, job postings, rejection letters, and business plans. The texts were written using Business English as a Lingua Franca and they had been prepared as part of a set of course units in Business Letter Writing and Business Marketing Writing taught in a Chinese university. Five of the business professionals were native speakers of English (four of American English, one of

Australian English) and three were Chinese non-native speakers of English (all fluent). The business professionals were asked the following questions:

1 What is your impression of the text?
2 Do you feel the text reads like professional writing? Why (not)?
3 What in the text (e.g. choice of words, expressions, sentence structures, rhetorical organization, content, etc.) conveyed the impression that you have about it?
4 If you were asked to revise the text, what changes would you make? Why?

(Zhang, 2013, p. 147)

Zhang created a coding system (based on Tardy, 2009) to categorize the business professionals' comments according to whether they referred to the formal aspects of the texts (formal), the process surrounding the writing (process), the rhetorical structure of the texts (rhetorical), or their content (subject-matter). The study showed that the business professionals commented on all four aspects of the texts, and unlike the observations made in the study by Seshadri and Theye (2000), they also commented on both the linguistic aspects of the text and on their transactional content – i.e. the way in which the content of the text related to the business context. Zhang also highlights the diverse nature of the comments provided by the business professionals, which he attributes to the variations that exist between different practices – and therefore different expectations – in business. The business professionals' evaluations can be summarized in five main ways:

1 The student writing was viewed in a positive way by the professionals, who commented in general that they understood what to write and how to write professionally.
2 The comments provided by the professionals were very diverse, even when they were considering writing produced by the same individual. One business professional made only three comments on the formal aspects of the writing of one of the students, compared to 86 comments made by another.
3 The professionals made comments across all four of the different categories (formal, process, rhetorical, subject matter), and although the majority of the comments related to the formal features of the writing and the subject matter that was included, both the process and rhetorical aspects of the texts were also discussed.
4 The detailed analysis that Zhang provides for each category shows that there were numerous differences between the ways in which the students wrote and the ways in which the professionals felt that they should have written. For instance, redundant language was frequently removed, boosters (e.g. using *exceptional* rather than *good*), were included, and negative messages were replaced with positive messages. Many of these comments and changes went far beyond the mechanics of grammar and style that are often the focus in teaching written Business English.

5 The professionals provided many illuminating comments on the lingua franca aspects of the texts. On the one hand, they identified aspects of the text such as accuracy, word meanings, and Chinglish in their comments on the formal characteristics of the students' writing, but on the other hand they also drew attention to the fact that they were interested in "mutual intelligibility rather than native-likeness" (Zhang, 2013, p. 152).

Zhang observes that the business professionals' comments point to the continuing gap between the classroom and the workplace. His analysis shows that these comments encompassed a wide variety of different topics, ranging from appropriate word choice, through the different ways in which business texts are disseminated, to the inclusion of particular content in a text to make it more effective. The variety of different comments also highlighted the intertwining of the Business English texts with business practices, and underlined the need to take real-life situations into account.

Zhang identifies three important pedagogical implications on the basis of his findings:

1 Business English education can – and should – equip students with a set of transferrable skills related to how different genres are used in the workplace.
2 Business English education should not be concerned with texts or interactions in isolation, but should take all the aspects of a text or spoken interaction into consideration, including the roles played by the people involved, the tasks they are carrying out as a result of that communication, and the variations that exist in different types of industry.
3 Business writing should be taught as if it is a business activity, and the production, distribution, and reception of texts should be contextualized within business and include reference to the formal, content, and rhetorical aspects of the text as well as to the processes surrounding it.

In an earlier publication, Zhang (2007) describes some of the ways in which the teaching of Business English has evolved in mainland China. In his discussion, he outlines the most recent developments in which Business English involves both a knowledge of business and a knowledge of Business English. In Part V, we look at this work in more detail.

Task 8.2 Developing a lesson to teach email communication

Consider the pedagogical implications for teaching Business English writing provided by Zhang (2013) that we have outlined above. Design a lesson to teach business email in which you take these observations, and any of the other ideas that you have read about in this chapter, into account.

Summary

In this chapter, we have looked at how an understanding of the context within which Business English texts originate and an understanding of how different audiences respond to texts can be incorporated into the classroom. We have looked specifically at two recent studies of prominent forms of computer-mediated written Business English, and we have also profiled a recent study that deconstructed potential differences between student business writing and writing by business practitioners. In the next two chapters (Part IV), we will continue to explore the modern business world and its impact on teaching Business English. Chapter 9 will focus on the related concepts of intertextuality and inter-discursivity and how these characterize Business English documents and spoken interactions, and Chapter 10 will consider new media and Business English, including social networking and the concept of multimodality. Both chapters will discuss how the interaction between spoken and written forms of communication can be incorporated in the Business English classroom.

Part IV

The Modern Business World

The Modern Business World

Chapter 9

Intertextuality and Interdiscursivity in Business English

Introduction

In the previous chapters, we looked at the studies of accounting and audit communication by Flowerdew and Wan (2006, 2010) and the studies of email by Evans (2012) and Gimenez (2014). All these studies identify the close relationship that exists between spoken and written forms of communication in business contexts – for example in the network of spoken and written references that occur in constructing an email, a tax letter, or an audit report, in the similarities that exist across different genres (even if they originated in different corporate settings), and in the relationship that can be traced between a document or a spoken interaction and the business goal that the writer or speaker is trying to achieve. In situations where a written text such as an audit report makes a reference to an additional written text such as the minutes of a meeting, or to a spoken event such as the meeting itself, we can refer to this as *intertextuality* because we can identify a cross-reference between two different texts or spoken events. In situations where a written text such as an email or a spoken interaction such as a negotiation facilitates the achievement of a corporate goal such as launching a new product or complying with a set of financial regulations, we can refer to this as *interdiscursivity*, where two sets of activities interact, because we can identify an interaction between the discourse activities in the email or the negotiation and the corporate activities required by doing business.

In this chapter, we further explore the intertextual and interdiscursive nature of Business English. We look at the interactions that researchers have identified between spoken and written forms of communication in the modern business world, together with the interactions between discourse activities and corporate activities, and we look at the consequences that these findings have for teaching Business English. We first focus on three researchers (Amy Devitt, Vijay Bhatia, and Leena Louhiala-Salminen) who pioneered the work on intertextuality and interdiscursivity in Business English. We will then profile the work of two scholars based in Hong Kong (Martin Warren and Winnie Cheng), who have taken an English for Specific Purposes approach in investigating the intertextual and interdiscursive references that business people working within specific professions make in the course of their work.

Research in intertextuality and interdiscursivity in Business English

One of the first accounts of intertextuality that looks at the interactions that take place across the business texts used within a specific professional community is Devitt's (1991) study of tax accounting texts. In this study, Devitt identifies three types of intertextuality in the texts used by tax accountants: generic intertextuality, referential intertextuality, and functional intertextuality. She describes these textual interactions as follows: "the types of texts (or genres) written by tax accountants (generic intertextuality); how these types use other texts (referential intertextuality); and how those types interact in the particular community (functional intertextuality)" (Devitt, 1991, p. 337).

As in the later studies of tax communication in Hong Kong by Flowerdew and Wan (2006, 2010) that we discussed in Part III of this volume, Devitt based her study on authentic texts, in this case collected from six large accounting firms in the US together with interviews with the tax accountants who were the users of those texts. Devitt found that although the texts had originated in different accounting firms, she could identify similar text types, or genres, that were used by all of them. For example, all six firms wrote letters to clients giving them an opinion, and five out of the six firms wrote letters to the tax authorities. The relationships between these similar types of texts, and the fact that they are easily recognizable as belonging to the same group of texts or genre even though they come from different corporations, is what Devitt refers to as *generic intertextuality*.

Devitt goes on to describe *referential intertextuality*, which is where there is a reference in one text to another text (such as a letter to a client that refers to the client's tax return), or where there is a reference in one text to a spoken event (such as when an internal memorandum refers to a meeting or a phone call). In her discussion on this type of intertextuality, Devitt observes that, "In some senses, not only does intertextuality help accountants to accomplish their work; intertextuality *is* their work" (Devitt, 1991, p. 342–43). In other words, without the continual cross-referencing from one text or spoken event to another, it would not be possible for the accountants to carry out their work activities. Devitt shows, for instance, that the tax accountants she studied made frequent explicit reference to general tax publications: across her corpus of 99 different types of written text, the writers made (on average) 1.47 references to tax documentation for every 200 words they wrote.

Finally, in her discussion on functional intertextuality, Devitt discusses the relationship between intertextuality and the professional community of tax consultants. She argues that the community can only exist because of the shared textual conventions that are recognized by all tax accountants as a result of generic intertextuality, combined with the shared knowledge that is maintained through the use of referential intertextuality between specific individual spoken events and written texts. In other words, without intertextuality, tax accountants would not be able to function as a community.

Later studies by researchers looking specifically at the use of Business English also show the crucial role played by generic and referential intertextuality in creating a community of business people. Akar and Louhiala-Salminen (1999), for instance, found similarities in business fax messages in English originating in two very different business contexts (Finland and Turkey) which suggested generic intertextuality across what was then a very new type of communication. They also identified numerous examples of referential intertextuality, with continual references not only to other texts or spoken events, but also to the specific activities that actually give form to the fax writers' business, such as the plans for a new product or the cancellation of an order. Likewise, Nickerson (2000) looks at internal corporate email in English at a multinational corporation and distinguishes between intertextual references to other communicative events or actions such as a fax or a meeting, and intertextual references to other corporate events or activities such as a corporate initiative on safety, the repair of a technical item, and the termination of a contract with a supplier. These early accounts of intertextuality in Business English are useful to revisit because they show the way in which writing and speaking facilitate the completion of corporate activities, foreshadowing later discussion on interdiscursivity.

In the next important study we look at in this chapter, Bhatia (2008) continues the discussion on the ways in which written texts and spoken events interact with the activities that a particular profession carries out. In this account, he argues that although researchers taking an English for Specific Purposes perspective have analyzed texts that occur within a particular professional context (as we have discussed earlier in this book), they have failed to take the professional practices that underpin these texts into consideration. As a result, many English for Specific Purposes researchers – and therefore also those teaching practitioners who have drawn on their work – have not gained sufficient understanding of how texts and spoken events are integrated with what people actually do. Bhatia (2008) refers to this integration as *interdiscursivity*; understanding the relationship between the discourse of professional communication, the activities or practices that people carry out to achieve their work aims, and the context or professional culture within which both take place. With respect to business people, this means investigating what happens in business writing or spoken events (as in an email or a departmental meeting), within a particular type of business organization with its own particular culture (such as at a multinational publishing house), and then understanding how organizational and textual features contribute to and interact with the corporation's activities (such as selling books, making a profit, retaining employees, etc.).

In Bhatia's (2008) terms, understanding interdiscursivity in Business English means understanding how business people use language as a resource to facilitate their activities, while at the same time drawing on their knowledge of what constitutes effective business practice and their knowledge of what their organizational (and/or professional) culture requires of them. Bhatia shows, for instance, how corporate disclosure documents like annual reports combine accounting information reporting financial facts with language that is typical of public relations in order to promote a positive image of the corporation. The writers of annual reports therefore use language as a resource, which allows them to present their corporation in a positive light in the text of the report, but they also use the financial data available for the corporation to provide additional evidence for their arguments. This is an example of an interdiscursive relationship between the language of public relations and the practice of reporting on financial performance. Bhatia (2008) argues that taking interdiscursivity into account is a useful way of bridging "the gap between the ideal world of the classroom and the real world of professional practice" (Bhatia, 2008, p. 171). Later in this chapter, we look at two Hong Kong studies that attempted to do that in order to equip Business English students to enter the workforce.

In the final study that we will look at in this section, we focus on Louhiala-Salminen's (2002) observational account of a Finnish business manager's discourse activities and how these were integrated into his working day. The study is notable because it was one of the first to try to understand the interactive and interdiscursive relationship between Business English and business life. In the study, Louhiala-Salminen observed a business manager at a multinational corporation and took note of his activities throughout one day. In addition, she recorded the spoken events that took place, collected copies of the written documentation that the manager used (both in reading and in writing), and followed up with interviews to contextualize what she had observed. The research was part of a larger project across four different countries that aimed to identify what business people needed to do with language or, in other words, why they needed to speak and write Business English. The project aimed to collect information in order to contribute to the creation of appropriate training materials for students at Business Schools located in different parts of the world (the US, the UK, Sweden, and Finland).

During the course of one day, Louhiala-Salminen shadowed the manager at the centre of her investigation, and completed an observation protocol designed to collect information on all the discourse activities that were related to each business activity: "time, participants, type of communication, purpose and type of discourse activity, and language" (Louhiala-Salminen, 2002, p. 214). In addition, she also noted anything else of interest, such as the use of intertextuality or the use of a particular style, and one day later she completed additional interviews with the manager, his superior, and subordinates, to put what she had found into context. In this way, the study included the (referential) intertextuality that Devitt (1991) had observed for tax accounting and the interdiscursivity that Bhatia (2008) would later identify as being crucial in understanding how language is used in business.

Over the course of the seven-hour observation period, Louhiala-Salminen identified 34 "discourse activities" with a clearly delineated beginning and end, all of which involved what she refers to as "interactional language use" (2002, p. 217), which meant that the manager was either engaged in talking or writing emails. Within these 34 activities, 14 mostly involved writing, 19 were mostly spoken, and one involved equal amounts of both speaking and writing. In addition, although there were more speaking activities overall, the total time used for writing activities was longer, and the manager moved from speaking to writing and vice versa throughout the day. Even more than a decade ago, Louhiala-Salminen observed that email played an important role in dictating the structure of the manager's day, in that he spent the first two hours of his day processing 95 new messages, after which most of the subsequent interactions that took place for the rest of the day were dictated either by what he had read in the morning or by additional incoming emails.

The detailed nature of Louhiala-Salminen's study meant that she was able to capture the corporate activities that the manager was facilitating through his use of spoken and written language. Therefore in addition to knowing that he used Finnish and English throughout the day, for instance, and in addition to detailing all the different business genres that he needed to use (email, phone conversation, face-to-face interaction, etc.), it was also possible to identify what he was trying to achieve – e.g. eliminating an accounting problem, understanding a new pricing system, updating inventories, developing a new project, etc. For example, in one discourse activity that lasted for 18 minutes, the manager attempted to understand more about a business problem involving a missing claim form. As a result, he engaged with written documentation in English while at the same time conducting a face-to-face discussion in Finnish. He then completed an email message in English to report on the conversation that he had just had in Finnish to try to find a solution for the problem. As in the case of Gimenez's (2014) study discussed in the previous chapter, this type of study provides us with invaluable information on the interdiscursive realities of the business world that we can then use to underpin our teaching materials. Even a short extract taken from Louhiala-Salminen's study would suggest that aspiring Finnish business people need to be able to switch constantly from one language to another (e.g. from Finnish to English), and to move rapidly between one mode of communication and another (e.g. between face-to-face discussion and email), while at the same time understanding the activities that are required in business organizations and the tasks that support them (for example, in collecting appropriate information, developing new products, maintaining good relationships with colleagues, problem-solving, etc.).

In addition to the complicated interdiscursive nature of the interactions that take place, Louhiala-Salminen (2002) also looks in detail at the (referential) intertextuality that characterized all of the discourse activities that took place. For instance, she describes a sequence of five different discourse activities (two phone calls and three email messages) taking place over a 33-minute period which attempted to facilitate a planned corporate procedure. In each case, there was explicit intertextual referencing to one or more previous spoken events or written texts, or to one or more future spoken events or written texts. She goes on to observe that sequences like this one occurred throughout the day, sometimes in parallel and sometimes in turn, with further intertextual connections between them adding to the complexity of both the discourse activities that took place as a result and the business tasks that underpinned them. She summarizes this as follows: "The discourse activities occurred in sequences that were interrelated and multimodal. Explicit intertextuality was characteristic of all messages and continuous cross-referencing between texts appeared" (2002, p. 224). Louhiala-Salminen comments that isolating reading, writing, speaking, and listening in the Business English classroom makes little sense, as she observed in her case study that these occurred simultaneously over the course of the manager's day in addition to rapid changes between languages, between speaking and writing, and between different business tasks. Like Gimenez (2014), she advocates using problem-based business cases as the most effective way of recreating the situations and skill sets (both business skills and communicative skills) that students are likely to need in real-life settings.

In the second part of this chapter, we go on to look at the work of several researchers in Hong Kong who have focused more recently on intertextuality and interdiscursivity in Business English in specific business contexts, and who have provided further insights as to how these should be incorporated into the classroom.

Task 9.1 Intertextuality and interdiscursivity in action

Look at the email message below, which is one of the email messages that Louhiala-Salminen collected during her observation period. Try to find as many examples of intertextuality and interdiscursivity as you can. Decide how you could use this type of analysis in teaching Business English.

Example 4. Email message from Timo to Domenico

Author: Timo Ranta at CB-Finland
Date 10.9.1997 15.15
To: Domenico Mintesanto at CB-Belgium cc: Dave Michell at CB-Belgium
cc: Timo Ranta at CB-Finland

To: Peter Boman at CB-Belgium
cc: Tero Karhu at Non-CB-Finland Subject: Re: cb 2345 disc space mgmnt

Hello Peter, Domenico,

thanks for your answer. I communicated the change of our IP-address to PTT.
The next thing they asked was that if the access is done via Lanlink or via Datanet. As
far as I understand they are two local public X.25 networks here in Finland: one is
owned by PTT and one by local telephone company.

I know that in the current setup brooc01 has an access to datanet in Finland. Is that
going to be true with ladybird socks-server, too? I mean: if we use socksifed ftp in
ladybird, will the traffic go out to the public network via socks-server somewhere in
Belgium?! And then we do not have any way of knowing how these files will be routed
in Finland via Datanet or via Lanlink). Please correct me if I have understood wrongly.

Best regards, Timo

(Louhiala-Salminen, 2002, p. 220–21)

Intertextuality and interdiscursivity in the classroom

Warren's (2013) study of intertextuality in the email messages used by two
business professionals in Hong Kong is an accessible account of Business
English use that could be adapted for the classroom. Drawing on previous
work by Bhatia (2004), Warren identifies four specific types of intertextuality:

1 a part of the text which explicitly refers to (i.e. signals) prior and/or
   predicted texts;
2 a part of a text which implicitly refers to (i.e. signals) prior and/or
   predicted texts;
3 text(s) which is/are embedded in a text by means of a paraphrase,
   summary, etc.;
4 text(s) which is/are embedded in a text by means of a direct quote (i.e. cut
   and pasted directly) from (an)other text(s) (Warren, 2013, p. 15).

In addition to these different types of referential intertextuality, Warren
investigated discourse flows, which means that he looked at how the messages
were connected with other messages or spoken events where the writers or
speakers made two or more, and often multiple, intertextual references. He
also identified the direction of the discourse flow, which meant that he looked at
whether the intertextual reference was made to a previous text or to a predicted,
possible text that had not yet been written.

The study was based on a corpus of 404 emails either received or written by
two professionals working in Hong Kong. One was an information technology
manager at a multinational bank and the other was a merchandiser for a
handbag manufacturer based in mainland China. The information technology
manager provided 271 emails and the merchandiser provided 133. These professionals were selected as part of a larger project investigating the communication

practices of six key sectors in the Hong Kong economy (see also later in this chapter for further discussion on this project) and also because they both carried out almost all of their professional communication through internal and external email and could therefore be usefully compared. In addition to collecting and analyzing the email data, Warren reports that discussions were held with both participants both before and after the data collection and analysis. Most importantly, the participants were asked to check the analyses to ensure that they made sense from a professional perspective. This interaction with the participants allowed Warren to identify 25 different discourse flows for each of the managers over the five-day data collection period.

Textbox 9.1 shows a seven-line example email taken from Warren's data in which he shows the presence of all four of the types of intertextuality that he focused on. The first type (Type 1) involved explicit references or signals to prior texts and/or predicted texts that are likely to occur in the future. These are shown in bold typeface in the example in Textbox 9.1, in lines 3, 4, and 5. The second type (Type 2) were implicit references or signals in the text to prior texts and/or predicted texts that are likely to occur in the future. These are shown in bold and underlined typeface in the Textbox example in line 6. The third type of intertextuality (Type 3) occurred when writers used paraphrases and summaries to refer to other texts, as is shown in italics in lines 4 and 5 in the example, and the final, fourth type of intertextuality (Type 4) occurred when writers used a direct quotation taken from another written or spoken text, as in line 5 in the example text, where the quotation is shown in italics and underlined.

Explicit references (Type 1) and paraphrases or summaries (Type 3) were the most frequent types of intertextuality that he found across all the data. On the other hand, although both the IT data and the merchandising data relied most on Type 1 intertextuality, the IT data tended to use more direct quotes (related to computer code), while the merchandising data used relatively more paraphrases and summaries. In addition, all the emails contained intertextual references, regardless of whether they originated in the IT profession or the merchandising profession. However, the discourse flows for the IT correspondence tended to point backwards to previous texts, whereas the discourse flows for the merchandising communication tended to point to future texts involving activities such as making enquiries or following up on an order. Warren's findings provide a clear indication that different professions may need to learn how to use different intertextual strategies in order to complete their work-related tasks.

Textbox 9.1 Intertextuality in email communication

5.2. Example 3

1. From: CXXXX
2. To: EXXXX; RXXXX; KXXXX
3. Subject: **Re: Re: lining**

4. **Just spoke to AXXXX, she said** *she has made a proposal to SXXXX, and waiting*
   for her
5. *decision,* **she sounds** *positive and* **mentioned** *about willing to make a "*<u>*win win situation*</u>*".*
6. **Let's see ...**
7. CXXXX

- Type 1s – explicit references (i.e. signals) to prior and/or predicted texts – are shown in bold.
- Type 2s – implicit references (i.e. signals) to prior and/or predicted texts – are shown in bold underlined.
- Type 3s – embedding by means of paraphrase, summary, etc. – are shown in italics.
- Type 4s – embedding in a text by means of direct quotes – are shown in italics underlined.

(Warren, 2013, p. 17)

In a classroom setting, looking at different types of referential intertextuality and considering whether these point forwards or backwards may raise students' awareness of the embedded nature of email communication and the highly networked nature of many Business English texts. Working with examples taken from authentic contexts would be a useful way to introduce this idea, together with a discussion on how the direction of the discourse flow may vary from one profession to another as a result of the different business activities that each profession carries out.

Finally in this chapter, we profile the study of communication in the land surveying profession in Hong Kong carried out by Cheng and Mok (2008), which investigates the communication processes and products that land surveyors need to complete their work-related tasks. The study focused on the work of the land-surveying department in a civil engineering consultancy firm, and was the result of the research collaboration between an English for Specific Purposes scholar (Cheng) and a land surveying scholar (Mok). This collaboration allowed the researchers to understand more about what we have referred to in this chapter as the interdiscursive relationship between the professional communication that takes place in a work context and the way in which that communication is used as a resource to facilitate work activities. As in many of the recent studies of how English is used in business contexts, Cheng and Mok (2008) combine several different methodologies in their study: survey research, the analysis of texts, and ethnography, which involved the same type of shadowing methodology that we discussed earlier in this chapter in Louhiala-Salminen's (2002) study of a Finnish manager. Land surveying is a key industry in Hong Kong and involves a wide variety of complex project management skills such as preparing proposals, scheduling projects, managing clients, conflict resolution, and staff development (Cheng & Mok, 2008). The study aimed to establish what it means to be discursively competent as a land surveyor in project management in Hong Kong by analyzing the flow of the communication that took place and the texts that were produced. As we will discuss below, understanding more about discursive competence is important, because it is only by being discursively competent that an individual can also develop professional expertise.

Cheng and Mok (2008) draw on the work of Capucho and Oliveira (2005) and of Bhatia (2004) to define discursive competence and the contribution that it makes to professional expertise. Discursive competence is defined as "the ability to understand and produce discourse in concrete situations", which means "the joint activation of three knowledge dimensions: linguistic, textual, and situational" (Capucho & Oliveira, 2005; cited in Cheng & Mok, 2008, p. 60). In other words, in a given situation, an individual must know what language they should use as well as what type of text (either spoken or written) they should produce. Following on from this, discursive competence is a key element in the development of professional expertise, alongside the development of discipline-specific knowledge and an understanding of what constitutes professional practice (Bhatia, 2004).

The researchers aimed to understand more about why land surveyors selected 1) the language that they did in a particular work situation (i.e. English or Cantonese), 2) the mode (i.e. spoken or written communication), and 3) the medium (i.e. telephone, video conference, face-to-face communication, computer-mediated communication, etc.). They also looked to see if there was a difference in the professional communication profiles of expert professionals compared to those of novice surveyors who were new to the profession, in an effort to identify any differences in their discursive competence. In order to do this, one of the research team members shadowed the 19 members of the Land Surveying Department at the consultancy firm over a period of six days. During that time, in addition to collecting examples of written documents, she took detailed notes on 1) how long a discourse event lasted, 2) overlaps with other discourse events, 3) the relationship between the participants involved, 4) the type of discourse event that occurred (for example, whether it was written or spoken, internal or external, etc.), and 5) the general language characteristics of the event (such as the medium used, whether there was any evidence of code-switching, etc.).

The findings of the study showed that the land surveyors needed to be able to write both specific types of documents such as tender invitations, and design plans and more general written communication such as emails and business letters. Without exception, all of these documents were written in English. While almost all of the internal spoken communication took place in Cantonese (including internal meetings, phone calls, and site inspections), most formal external meetings took place in English because of the presence of non-Cantonese speaking participants. Cheng and Mok (2008) describe a commonly occurring situation in which an external contact phones the department in Cantonese to clarify the details on the project. Although the phone call takes place predominantly in Cantonese, English is also used during the discussion to make intertextual references to previous texts and to talk about technical terms. A formal written record of the call is then made in English to pass on to another department, and the response from that department is then relayed back formally in writing in English to the external contact. In addition, the written communication is characterized by large numbers of referential intertextual references, such that in one 121-word text which was an official query (a formal request to clarify information), there were ten intertextual references, six referring to one specific text and four referring to four additional previous texts. Finally, the study also revealed major differences in the discourse tasks carried out by the senior surveyors when compared to the junior surveyors. For instance, whereas the junior surveyors spent as much as 80% of their time on fieldwork and as little as 20% in the office, the senior surveyors could spend as much as 100% of their time in the office with no fieldwork at all. Consequently, the senior surveyors were also much more likely to conduct their business in writing (and then in English), whereas the junior employees were much more likely to be engaged in the speaking activities related to fieldwork (which would take place almost exclusively in Cantonese).

Cheng and Mok's study shows how the interdiscursivity that existed between the discoursal activities and the surveyors' business activities affected the choices they made in terms of the mode they selected, the genre they chose, the language they needed to use, and the amount and type of intertextual references they required. The findings also revealed that progress in a Hong Kong surveyor's career greatly impacts their discourse tasks, with particular reference to how much Business English they need and what they need it for. The insights provided by the study could be used to inform the development of appropriate Business English teaching and training materials for other professional settings. In Part V of this volume, we look at several studies that were also completed in Hong Kong (e.g. Bremner, 2008, 2010; Lam et al., 2014 in order to compare the findings of studies into workplace Business English with the materials that are designed to teach it.

Task 9.2 Developing teaching materials on intertextuality and interdiscursivity

Talk to a business person you know who needs to use English as part of their daily life.

1 Make a list of the sorts of things that you would need to find out about if you were going to design a training course on Business English for one of their junior colleagues in order to develop their language skills in an appropriate way for the future. Think about how you might find out about them. What would you need to do?

2 Using the examples taken from the studies we have discussed in this chapter to help you, ask your informant to identify some specific examples of intertextuality and interdiscursivity that you could use as the basis for a set of teaching materials.

Summary

In this chapter, we have considered the important role played by intertextuality and interdiscursivity in the English used by specific business professions. We have focused on a number of studies that have looked in detail at the relationships that exist across different texts and spoken events, and at the inter-relationship between discourse tasks and business tasks. The studies we have showcased have highlighted the variations that may exist in how specific professions use Business English and how the way in which it is used may change as a person becomes more senior. In the next chapter, we look at the impact of new media on the business world in general, and on the workplace context and discourse activities in which Business English is used in particular. In light of technological developments in business communication, we consider the need to promote Business English students' familiarity with new (and social) media, as well as their use in discourse activities in which Business English is used, and we suggest a number of ways in which both might be achieved in the Business English classroom.

Chapter 10

New Media and Business English

Introduction

In the previous chapter, we considered intertextuality and interdiscursivity, or how different spoken and written forms of communication interact to allow users of Business English to realize discourse activities (e.g. in emails or presentations) that in turn support and realize corporate activities (e.g. launching a new product). Earlier in this book, in Parts II and III, we saw how business professionals use Business English to get their work done on a daily basis in a variety of settings using different genres such as meetings, negotiations, emails, and reports. What this demonstrates above all is that the workplace is a complex communicative space in which business people use not only a variety of traditional genres and communication forms (e.g. letters, reports, and phone calls) but increasingly also newer media (e.g. email, instant messaging, and websites). In addition, they have at their disposal social media and social networking sites (SNSs) including Twitter, Instagram, LinkedIn, and Facebook.

Social media are computer-based, digital applications or technological tools that allow individual users to join communities of like-minded people online and then generate (i.e. produce and upload) their own content to share with others. Social media involve user-generated content and collaboration and interaction among users. As more and more users worldwide communicate and engage with one another in this way, businesses are increasingly seeking to employ social media effectively in order to support and realize corporate activities. For example, they use social media to engage online with consumers for marketing research, with potential employees (as part of the recruitment process), and with stakeholders more generally (e.g. investors, consumers, and the general public) to support their public relations strategy.

Social media platforms are particularly useful in international business communication contexts because they can support global work teams that need to collaborate on projects over long distances (for example through Yammer, a social networking platform for organizations), facilitate marketing activities involving consumers in different countries (for example real-time marketing through Twitter), or allow corporate communication messages to reach widely dispersed stakeholder groups located around the world (for example through the corporate website). As new media are increasingly being integrated into the communication and media mix that organizations use to do business, it is important that students of Business English become familiar with new and emerging media, how they are employed by businesses to support communication functions, and how to use them to support business-related tasks and activities. The latter in particular could be realized in the Business English classroom through the implementation of relevant, real-life task-based activities involving newer media.

In this chapter, we consider the need for multimedia literacy in business communication and offer some suggestions as to how this could be promoted in the Business English classroom. We feature a number of studies that have thrown light on Business English students' needs and employers' requirements for computer-mediated communication skills in their future employees, and we consider the multimodal nature of new media, which more often than not combine visual resources (e.g. charts, photos, and video) and textual resources or 'modes', and sometimes aural (i.e. audio) resources as well (for example on corporate websites or social networking sites such as Facebook). In doing so, we will explore how task-based activities in the Business English classroom might incorporate new media, including social media.

The need for multimedia literacy

In Chapter 8, we looked at work by Evans (2010, 2012) and Gimenez (2006, 2014) that takes an English for Specific Purposes approach and focuses on how the relatively new medium of email is integrated into the real-life business context. Their studies clearly show how email permeates all aspects of business life, plays a crucial role in both the internal and external communication of organizations, and interfaces with other forms of spoken or written communication. As we also saw in Chapter 8, email is rarely produced in isolation, but is more often part of a chain of messages; and it rarely constitutes a discrete form of communication but more often than not operates in combination with other forms of communication (e.g. phone calls or meetings) in the business context. Evans in particular notes that email has received surprisingly little attention in both business textbooks and Business English textbooks to date. Nevertheless, both Evans and Gimenez suggest that email should play a substantial role in Business English courses, and that it is best taught as part of near-authentic, task-based simulations that involve a re-creation of the activities surrounding business emails, and thus focus on more than just the Business English writing skills needed to produce a single email message. Evans suggests that such simulations should ideally be multimodal as well, in the sense that they should involve multiple modes of communication (reading, writing, listening, and/or speaking), and that they should be embedded in other important forms of business communication such as negotiations, presentations, and reports. This would allow students to train not only their language skills (e.g. their command of grammar, vocabulary, and register) but also their strategic communication competence as future business professionals who will need to deal with different forms of communication, decide which form or forms are more or less suitable in a particular business situation and business activity, and who will very often need to juggle more than one communication form at the same time.

The need to communicate various messages simultaneously at work is particularly evident from the study of multimedia use in the workplace by Gimenez (2014), which we discussed at some length in Chapter 8. His study of multi-communication, that is, of how people engage in and maintain multiple business conversations at the same time, often through the use of different media (e.g. email, instant messaging, and telephone), showed that business people, in the interests of efficiency and speed, frequently multitask when communicating at work without this causing communication breakdowns. On the basis of his observations and findings, Gimenez suggests that Business English classroom activities should aim to sensitize students to the multimedia demands of the modern business world, should be designed in such a way as to simulate realistic business situations that require students to use Business English in different media and genres, and should require the multitasking and simultaneous conversations which are characteristic of the real-life business contexts in which they will find themselves in after graduation. Beyond providing training in their use of Business English in a near-realistic business context and for business-related tasks, such classroom activities would increase students' awareness of the different media they are likely to have at their disposal in the workplace, how these media interface with one another (and more traditional media and genres), and how different media might be used in combination (or "packed", in Gimenez's words) to realize a particular business task effectively. As a result, the integrated, multimodal, multimedial tasks such as those suggested by both Evans and Gimenez (see Chapter 8) would also go some way to increasing Business English students' multimedia literacy.

To further illustrate how new media and communication technologies influence business and work, we profile two further studies from the field of business communication that investigated to what extent business people adopt and use new technologies (Turner et al., 2010) and that gauged employers' views of the computer-mediated communication skills needed by potential employees (Jones, 2011). While neither of these studies is specifically related to Business English, they do, however, provide valuable insights into how new technologies are used within the workplace. We begin with Turner et al. (2010), who investigated communication practices in a small US company. They used interviews and two surveys a year apart to investigate whether employees adopted new technologies such as Twitter, instant messaging, social networking sites, and blogging, and how much they used them. The researchers also wanted to determine to what extent such new media were replacing traditional media in the workplace. They conducted their study in a relatively small company (around 50 employees), as this type of company makes up more than 85% of all US businesses, and also because a higher proportion of employees were likely to be able to participate in this type of study than would be the case in a larger company, thus providing a clearer picture of the small company's overall communication pattern. The two surveys, conducted in May 2008 and May 2009, enabled the researchers to obtain an understanding of the mix of communication tools employees used and adopted over time. A few months after the second survey, they held in-depth interviews with a number of the participants in the second survey. The participants in the study were all highly educated knowledge workers (employees and contractors) who used computers at work on a daily basis. They usually worked in teams and on a number of projects simultaneously, although project team members might vary from one project to the next. All employees occupied offices on the same floor. Some teams also included colleagues from other organizations, often located in another country. The study involved three different processes: an analysis of the media adopted and used at work, an analysis of patterns of behavior across users, and an exploration of the strengths and weaknesses attributed by the employees to these technological tools.

As in the Evans and Gimenez studies referred to before, Turner et al.'s study showed that email was prevalent in the workplace and was a preferred method of communication for the employees. In terms of popularity, email competed closely with face-to-face communication. An important strength attributed to email was that the process of composing an email allowed writers to "sort out their thinking", resulting in a clearer message. Although the process of composing email may take time, causing delays in communication, respondents nonetheless regarded the time it took as a valuable aspect of email, for knowledge workers in particular. In addition to email, frequently used media included phone, notes, and face-to-face communication. As expected by the authors, no differences were found in the use of these relatively traditional media over the course of a year (from Survey 1 to Survey 2). With respect to emerging media, however, employees reported that they used instant messaging, blogging, and virtual worlds such as Second Life more often in 2009 than in 2008. In addition, more people used instant messaging and virtual worlds at work than in their personal life. Their use of wikis did not change between 2008 and 2009.

Task 10.1 Multimedia use in the workplace

Talk to a business person you know who needs to use English to communicate at work on a regular basis. Find out:

- what media they use at work, and what business-related tasks they use them for (keep in mind the distinction between the traditional and newer, social, media discussed in this chapter and elsewhere);

- which media they consider most effective for work-related tasks and why, and which media they consider less effective for work-related tasks and why;
- whether they consider their English to be different when using new media (versus more traditional media), and if so, in what way(s) they consider it to be different. Do they adapt their English in any way when using new (versus traditional) media?;
- whether they ever experience challenges when using new media or English in new media, and if so, what these challenges are.

Based on the information you have gathered, which new media might you incorporate in an activity/simulation for the Business English classroom? Write a brief outline for such an activity/simulation.

Turner et al. (2010) found that employees were not adopting new media (such as Twitter, blogs, and social networking sites) in place of existing communication forms over time (i.e. from Survey 1 to Survey 2). Instead, new, emerging media were being used next to, and in combination with, existing media. Certain media were regarded as effective for a particular type of communication, and employees chose the technology or application that best suited the task or activity at hand. Instant messaging, for instance, was not found to be replacing email or face-to-face communication. Instead, it seemed to have found a niche in support of a specific type of communication that took place frequently in the company, namely long-distance project team meetings. The authors note that blogs and social networking sites seem to allow employees to virtually move outside the small organization and connect with other information sources and other professionals. Blogs, in particular, were used to communicate ideas (in response to other blog posts) to colleagues and people outside the company. Many of the respondents in Turner et al.'s study used the professional social networking site LinkedIn to maintain business contacts, but they reported that such platforms also provide the possibility to interact socially with colleagues inside and outside the company. In this respect, because new media are collaborative – sharing information and opinions is central to their 'social' nature – they extend professional communication beyond the organization itself. In this way, new media are used in a business context as a means or a tool to build professional relationships as well.

The second study we profile was conducted by Jones (2011), who considered the need for computer-mediated skills in employees by investigating employers' expectations of entry-level employees' communication skills within the specific context of the accounting sector. Jones argues that communication skills in general (i.e. for speaking and writing business activities) are considered to be an essential requirement for accounting professionals, noting that the American Institute of Certified Public Accountants considers communication to be an essential competency that all students training to be accountants need to develop (Jones, 2011, p. 247). As part of overall communication competency, Jones notes that effective business writing is most often singled out as the core requirement, but that it is unclear from the literature what exactly this entails. Furthermore, he suggests that little is known about the employer's perspective on what communication skills are important for (selecting) employees, and what is known tends to be about traditional communication (e.g. written reports, oral presentations) rather than new, computer-mediated communication skills such as microblogging or social networking. It is also as yet unclear to what extent new media (including social media) are beginning to replace the traditional media used in the business context, in the same way that email communication overtook fax communication in the 1990s. The study aimed to investigate this in more detail.

Jones conducted an online survey of employers who had hired or who intended to hire accounting graduates from California State University, Northridge, where he was employed at the department of Business and Economics. Of the 444 firms he approached, 12.4% (56 respondents) filled in the survey. The survey aimed to identify employer priorities with regard to the writing skills new employees require, as well as whether new employees actually have the skills that are required. To this end, employers were asked to rate a total of 26 written skill competencies which were drawn up from a review of the literature and supplemented with a set of emerging computer-mediated communication skills (see below, under point 4). The respondents rated the 26 skills with respect to 1) how important they regarded each skill to be for new employees, and 2) how satisfied they were with new employees' levels of competence in each skill. Based on the scores assigned, and to simplify the analysis, the skills were grouped into four overarching categories (Jones, 2011, pp. 260–61), as follows:

1   Basic writing mechanics:

- produces correctly spelled documents
- uses grammar correctly
- uses effective business vocabulary
- punctuates documents properly.

2   Documentation:

- prepares concise, accurate documents, supportive of the subject matter
- cross-references and reaches conclusions in complete and accurate manner
- properly cites references to literature and other sources.

3   Effective writing:

- organizes information into effective sentences and paragraphs
- writes clearly and precisely
- edits and revises conscientiously

- organizes, develops, and composes effective reports
- creates document drafts using word processor
- employs appropriate level of tone and formality
- writes naturally and at the reader's level
- provides effective transitions between ideas
- writes persuasively
- formats letters and memos properly
- writes routine letters (e.g. requests, inquiries, etc.)
- incorporates headings and structural cues to guide reader
- includes well-designed illustrations, graphs, tables
- outlines materials before writing
- uses jargon in appropriate situations.

4 Computer-mediated communication:

- effectively uses email for external and internal correspondence
- maintains a professional presence on social networks
- uses instant/text messaging effectively
- narrates blog and microblog entries (e.g. tweets) in readable style.

Jones' study provides an indication as to what employers regard as essential communication skills (and shortcomings) for entry-level employees. Overall, the employers regarded skills that were clustered in the category 'Basic writing mechanics' as most important, with a mean score of 4.53 on a seven-point scale. The categories 'Documentation' and 'Effective writing' were ranked second and third in terms of relative importance, with mean scores of 4.39 and 4.08 respectively. Finally, the category 'Computer-mediated communication' ranked lowest in importance (mean: 3.15), and the difference between this and the other three categories was statistically significant. It should be noted, however, that two communication skills that involve multimodal communication skills, namely 'incorporates headings and structural cues to guide reader' and 'includes well-designed illustrations, graphs, tables' (that is, skills that require the effective integration of visual and textual modes) are subsumed under the category 'Effective writing', which was ranked the third most important cluster of skills. Although 'Computer-mediated communication' was ranked as the least important of the four categories of communication skills, Jones observes that its mean score shows that it was still regarded as a communication skills category that was "important" for entry-level employees (the other categories were seen as "very important" to "extremely important").

The second question Jones investigated was to what extent potential employers viewed new employees as possessing the different skills distinguished in the study. Overall, he found that employers took a neutral stance with regard to the level of competence displayed in these skills by new accounting employees, and that this was the case for the majority of the 26 skills distinguished – including the skills clustered under computer-mediated communication. Means for 'satisfaction with entry level employees' competence' centred around the neutral midpoint of the scale (neither satisfied nor dissatisfied) for all the communication skills distinguished, and there was only one skill with which employers were actually satisfied, namely 'Ability to draft documents using a word-processor' (mean: 4.21). Overall, employers were least satisfied with potential employees' communication competence in the areas of 'Clear writing' and 'Outlining'. On the whole, then, the employers in the study were not overly impressed by the communication skills displayed by entry-level employees in accounting positions.

What Jones' study shows is that computer-mediated communication skills are indeed regarded by employers as important, although seemingly less so – at least at the time of the study (ca. 2010) – than basic writing mechanics, and documentation and effective writing skills. At the same time, the same employers were not satisfied (but 'neutral') with regard to entry-level employees' computer-mediated communication skills, which suggests that there is room for improvement in this area of communication as well as in the other areas investigated in the study. In the same way that both Gimenez and Evans recommend embedded, multimedial task-based business simulations for the Business English classroom in order to create an authentic learning environment, Jones suggests that communication classes aimed at simulating real-life practice would be well advised to incorporate tasks that train students' communication skills in the context of new and emerging media (instant messaging, Twitter, blogging, etc.), at least in training courses for accountants. Such a recommendation could clearly be extended to the Business English classroom, in situations where students could train their communication skills – including computer-mediated communication skills – in order to conduct the business needed by various specific professions. In future research taking an English for Specific Purposes approach, it would be useful to know more about which new media are in use in a particular profession and how such media interact with other traditional forms of communication, and it would also be useful to map the specific skill sets that an individual requires to use both types of media effectively.

In the next section, we will profile two studies that provide examples of how new media can be incorporated into the Business English classroom and allow students to combine their acquisition of language skills and communicative competence with the strategies they also need to be successful in the business world.

New media and new technology in the Business English classroom

In their pioneering account of a website project used as part of a Business English course for second-year students of International Business Communication at a Dutch university, Planken and Kreps (2006) provide a rare example of a task-based, business-related project that revolves around the design and construction of a multimodal communication medium, namely an organizational website. As early as 2006, the authors signalled the need to keep up with technological developments in business communication in the real world by creating a Business English classroom environment in which students can learn to create and evaluate communication "within a fluid, multimedia landscape" (p. 421). They note that in the five years before their account of the website project was published, the courses in which they taught Business English had already shifted their emphasis from how to write effective, reader-oriented business texts in traditional business genres (e.g. letters, memos, and reports) to "the effective design [...] of business messages that are highly visual, screen-based, and communicated in hybrid or emergent genres still being shaped by electronic media such as email, PowerPoint and hypertext" (p. 421). They noted that the high degree of multimodality associated with new, digital communication environments such as websites (in which text, graphics, visuals, sound, and animations can be combined to create the message, and which can feature or integrate software applications such as email, online surveys, and chat as well as links to other media such as Twitter, Youtube, Facebook, and Instagram) meant that the means professionals have at their disposal to create messages and design information have dramatically increased. As a result, writing had become an increasingly creative and complex undertaking. For example, in addition to creating an effective message in terms of content (that is, in terms of a message that is reader-oriented and fulfils the reader's information needs), web-mediated messages (for example, on corporate websites and blogging sites) also require effective design with regard to the way in which the textual and visual content is presented. Planken and Kreps suggest that writers of web-based messages must therefore take various design aspects into account. These include whether the overall structure in which the information is presented (e.g. a website) is easy to navigate, and whether the layout of webpages on which information is presented is user-friendly (for example, easy to find and pleasant on the eye in terms of colours, font, etc. used). Also, the information itself should be easy to skim for users reading from the screen rather than on paper; for example it should be clearly structured, with the main points presented up front, simple syntax, keywords highlighted, and clear subheadings pointing to content ahead, etc.

The website project Planken and Kreps describe was part of a second-year English for Specific Business Purposes writing course at university for non-native (Dutch) users of English (see Planken et al., 2004, for a description of the Business English programme that featured this course). The business writing course – and the website project within it – extended over 14 weeks (one semester). Students met in the classroom or computer lab for two hours a week. The website project required them to take on the role of communication consultants (working in teams of two to three students), and to design and implement a new website section consisting of six hyperlinked webpages of information, within an existing organizational website. The webpages were to be clearly multimodal, incorporating at least textual and visual content and with the potential to also include other media such as audio and video, etc. Because the writing course (and the International Business Communication programme it was part of) was largely (90%) attended by female students at the time, Planken and Kreps chose an existing organizational website and an existing organization that would be likely to appeal to the students, namely the website of a UK-based association for female entrepreneurs. This non-profit organization aimed to promote female entrepreneurship and offered an online community as well as information, coaching, and mentoring for UK business-women. Within the website project, the students' task was to design and create content for a new section of the existing website aimed specifically at female university graduates who wanted to start up a company. In this way, the assignment required the student consultancy teams to collaboratively create web-based, multimodal content as communication consultants, geared to a target group (young female graduates), in a setting they could identify with. The website section was to be implemented as a functioning (online) hypertext with working links, etc. A description of the website project is provided in Textbox 10.1.

In Phase one, students studied relevant introductory texts, background articles, and usability studies, which they presented and discussed in the first four class sessions. For example, they studied and discussed an article by Spyridakis (2000) on the differences between reading from the screen versus reading from paper, and research-based guidelines for creating effective web content. They also considered Harrison's (2003) account of the different ways in which images can support text to create meaning and bring about different reader effects, and Tovey's (1998) article on hypertext structures and effective information design. The aim of this orientation phase was to make students more aware of the constraints imposed on people's information-processing capacity when they read information from a screen rather than from paper. These constraints create web-based readers who, for example, process 'chunks' of information and skim and skip text (rather than read word-for-word). They also create impatient readers who expect important information up-front or in bulleted lists rather than complete sentences.

In the orientation phase, it was important that the students became aware of web readers' processing limitations and subsequent reading behaviour so that they could take this into account when designing multimodal content for their website section, like web writers would do in real life. In the orientation phase, students also discussed whether web writing and web design guidelines presented as best practice (see e.g. Morkes & Nielsen, 1997; US Department of Health and Human Services, n.d.) were reflected in two existing websites, which they analyzed and assessed with regard to overall design, textual and visual content, and usability. Their findings were presented in a business report for the client, and their analysis served as a basis for recommendations with regard to the website section they were to design and implement for the project. In this way, the students were encouraged in their design team (in team meetings, with agendas and minutes) to consider how guidelines and best practices they had observed in existing, comparable websites might be applied in their own project. They were asked to focus specifically on the interaction of text, visuals, and hyperlinks (i.e. internal links within webpages and between webpages within a website, and external links to other websites), and implications for reader appeal, clarity of information, and navigability.

In the second half of the course (six weeks), students created and implemented the actual website section (see Textbox 10.1, Stage 2). In weekly, two-hour workshops, they were taught the rudiments of hypertext markup language (HTML) using a freeware HTML editor they downloaded from the internet and installed at home. The workshops were supported by an online tutorial, created and maintained by the course instructors, which students could access via the university's website. During the second half of the course, students regularly received feedback on the webpages they were creating with regard to "overall design, relevance, clarity, and completeness, interaction and balance between text and visuals, usability, English, and so on" (2006, p. 425). At the end of the course, the teams presented their website section in a final Power-Point presentation for the theoretical client. They also submitted a business report addressed to the client, which accompanied the finished website and set out the motivation for and aims behind its design, content, navigation, and information structure.

Textbox 10.1 A description of a website project

Assignment. You are working at the British Association of Women Entrepreneurs (BAWE), a non-profit organization that promotes the growth of female-owned businesses in the UK. BAWE is planning a new initiative aimed at female university graduates who want to start up their own businesses. BAWE wants to create a separate section on its existing website geared to this target group.

Stage 1: Orientation. You are responsible for the design and content of the new website section. As a first step in this creative process, you've been asked to submit a report analyzing and assessing two existing websites that offer start-up information to female entrepreneurs (SCORE and Womenowned). Your brief is to see who creates effective web content and to establish what information design features might be effective for the new website section you will create.

Stage 2: Design and implementation. Your section of the BAWE website should contain the following: 1) an introductory web page, 2) start-up information for young female entrepreneurs, 3) what BAWE can offer, 4) facts and figures, 5) useful links, 6) a web page of your own choosing. Information should be relevant, up-to-date, and useful.

Assessment. Your final grade will be based on the report of your analysis of two US-based comparable websites for female entrepreneurs (30%), and the section of the BAWE website you implemented, including a report in which you motivate your design and content to the client (70%). These aspects will be considered in the assessment of the website section:

- The language used should be yours, not copied.
- The language used should be of an acceptable standard with regard to punctuation, spelling, grammar, vocabulary, tone, style, etc.
- Color scheme and visuals should be appropriate for the client; indicate copyright holders for borrowed images.
- Visuals should complement, illustrate or support textual elements.
- Graphics/buttons should have a clear function.
- Page/section content should be relevant.
- Page/section layout should be appropriate and consistent.
- All hyperlinks and any forms you include should work.
- Length of time to load should be reasonable.
- The section should be easy to navigate (and topical information should be easy to find).
- An email link to the client needs to be included.
- The section should contain both external and internal links.
- The overall look and feel should be professional and complementary to the rest of the site.

(Planken & Kreps, 2006, 423–24, slightly adapted)

The website project described by Planken and Kreps is a useful example of a task-based assignment for the Business English classroom that involves multiple, interrelated media and communication forms such as team meetings, presentations, emails, business reports and websites and mimics, to some degree at least, the intertextual and interdiscursive nature of real workplace communication (see Chapter 9). Furthermore, the project centres around computer-mediated business communication (websites and website content), which was still a relatively new type of business communication at the time of the study, and it makes use of authentic business information and Business English samples (e.g. from existing organizational websites) relating to a situation the students in the course could easily identify with (female start-ups). Finally, the project aimed to encourage students to gain greater awareness of (and to learn to apply) research-based insights on usability, web design, web-writing guidelines, and multimodal meaning-making (i.e. the way visual and textual information work together to create a message), all of which are essential in creating effective web-based business communication. In a project such as this, students not only work with – and on – their Business English in a near-realistic, business-relevant task, but they also become familiar with related areas of knowledge and practice that are essential if they are to function as informed, media literate communicators in a multimedial and multimodal work environment.

Task 10.2 Multimodality on corporate websites

Visit the corporate website of a well-known company, organization or institution that operates internationally. The website you choose should be in English (or at least partly in English); potential examples would be Cocacola.com, Shell.com, Honda.com, Gillette.com, Starbucks.com, Hilton.com, BMW.com, etc. Analyze the homepage/main page with regard to the following:

Multimodality. What modalities create the message? How do the different modalities support each other to create the message? Which are dominant and which seem subordinate?

Multimedia. Does the homepage integrate other media (Twitter, email, online forms, etc.)? Why does it do this?

Textual content. What do you notice about the textual content and the way it is presented and structured? How would you characterize the Business English used on the website? Formal/informal? Conversational? Informative/promotional? Is this similar (or not) to the way Business English is used in/on other media?

The second study we briefly discuss reports on a classroom project in which Facebook was integrated as a teaching/learning resource in an intermediate foreign language learning class, in this case French. Although this case study does not feature Business English, we feel that the teaching/learning resource investigated could easily be integrated into a Business English course. (We discuss this further later on.) The study, conducted by Blattner and Lomicka in 2012, aimed to investigate how students would respond to the use of a social networking tool to promote second language learning, and to examine students' attitudes to using a social networking tool like Facebook in an academic, learning setting, rather than for social purposes. The study observed and surveyed 24 students enrolled in an intermediate level French course at a US university. A Facebook group page was created for the course, and students were to use the group page to take part in regular discussions on a number of set themes (nine in total) that corresponded to their coursebook. Students also used Twitter, email, and Skype to promote different types of written and oral communication in the foreign language, and to extend the discussions beyond the classroom should they wish to do so. The 24 US students in the study were simultaneously engaged in an exchange with students in France, and they used Facebook at least twice a month to take part in discussions in both their first language (English), and the foreign language (French). A question or statement on a particular theme was posted by the teacher and students were given a week to respond. To create a response of at least 50 words and in an effort to promote a degree of autonomy in the language learning process, students were encouraged to search for, select, and analyze relevant sources on the themes on their own. The goals for using Facebook as part of the course were:

- to develop linguistic competencies;
- to exchange views on cultural topics;
- to build a sense of community among the exchange students in France and the US;
- to extend learning beyond the classroom.

The study found that on the whole the students responded fairly positively to Facebook as a tool for language learning. They were interested in what their classmates posted and tended to log in on a daily basis to follow the discussions on course-related themes. In the view of the researchers, the Facebook context created a social experience that facilitated intercultural communication and language practice in their own and in the foreign language for the students. Students enjoyed the discussions on French culture through Facebook and other media, and they enjoyed posting reactions in both their own and the foreign language. The majority of students reported that they felt they had learned from their French classmates, that they enjoyed interacting with 'real' native speakers of the target language, and that they were interested in hearing about themes from a French perspective. At the end of the course, they felt more comfortable about posting their ideas and opinions publicly within the course environment, and said that they planned to continue to communicate with local classmates on Facebook and other social media, and to a lesser extent with their French counterparts.

According to the researchers, Facebook can connect classmates both socially and academically, and can extend the language-learning environment beyond the classroom. Only very few students surveyed commented that Facebook was perhaps not suitable for classroom activities all the time because it was seen as too personal. Nonetheless, the students certainly seem to have applied themselves in doing the Facebook assignments, as the authors note that students' posts were consistently "meaningful, because they have a real audience with whom they communicate" (p. 14). The learners themselves also recognized that Facebook helped them to put their developing foreign language skills to use as they engaged in authentic exchanges with real people, which is essential to developing communicative competence. Based on their observations and survey findings, Blattner and Lomicka suggest that social networking services like Facebook can be used in language learning courses as an extension of the classroom, so that students can continue to develop their language competence "in a fun environment" (p. 16).

This case study required students to engage in discussion on set themes relating to the specific course materials, and this could easily be extended to business-related themes (e.g. leadership, business culture, the economy, entrepreneurship, etc.) in a Business English classroom setting. A similar Facebook format integrated in a Business English course can encourage students to gain a better understanding of sociocultural norms in target countries where the language is spoken, and can allow them to develop a broader perspective on the business world. Although the students in this case study were learning French as a foreign language, a Facebook assignment such as this can just as usefully be integrated in an English course. Finally, by setting assignments like this, in which students are required to find and consult secondary sources of information in order to respond meaningfully to set themes, students can be exposed to real-life business language in use, which provides valuable input for their language learning process.

In the next chapter, we will explore other approaches to teaching business language, including blended and mobile learning in the Business English classroom (see for example Rapanta et al., 2014).

Summary

In this chapter, we have considered how the increased availability and use of new and emerging media have changed the environment in which business people work and communicate. We have explored some of the ways in which new technologies have impacted on the workplace and on business communication practices. We noted that, as a result, and if students are to be prepared adequately for professional life, Business English teaching and training materials should reflect the complexity of doing business by incorporating task-based activities that are both multimedial and multimodal. In other words, teaching materials need to integrate different forms of communication as well as multiple media and technological tools. This would increase students' awareness of the new media available to them and their awareness of how such media interface with one another and with traditional media. Classroom assignments and task-based simulations could help train students not only to use Business English in the context of new media, but also to use such media within a Business English workplace setting.

In the next part of this book, we look in more detail at teaching approaches and Business English, followed by a discussion on course design, task design, and the creation of specific teaching materials.

Part V

Learners, Teachers, and Materials

Chapter 11

Teaching Approaches and Business English

Introduction

In this chapter, we consider some of the teaching approaches discussed by researchers in English for Specific Purposes that teachers can usefully incorporate into their Business English courses. We show how these can be used to meet the needs of different types of learners, particularly in mixed proficiency classrooms, and suggest how one of these approaches in particular (team-teaching) can help teachers of Business English who do not have an extensive knowledge of business.

In the discussion that follows, we consider three English for Special Purposes approaches to teaching that could be adapted, individually or in combination, to a Business English teacher's own contexts in order to create an appropriate learning environment. We look at project-based learning, team-teaching, and blended learning, and illustrate each of these with a number of examples taken from different teaching environments, where they have been used with very different types of students.

Project-based learning

Project-based learning aims to promote learning by doing and is an alternative to teacher-led classroom learning. Students work on a larger project in order to apply the knowledge they have acquired and to realize a series of practical tasks and assignments. Project-based learning is therefore a complex form of task-based learning, in that students generally need to complete a set of shorter integrated tasks, all of which contribute to the completion of a wider project. For example, the launch of a new product (project) may require 1) a team meeting to discuss the initial design of the product (task), 2) an email simulation to refine the design (task), 3) a team presentation to introduce the product (task), and 4) a report to summarize the new product details (task). In addition, because students work in groups to realize the project, this approach is highly collaborative and communicative and therefore ideally suited for integration into communication or language learning courses.

Within the context of language teaching, project-based learning has been characterized by Stoller (2006) as follows: it integrates a variety of individual and collaborative skills; develops students' understanding of a topic or specialism through the integration of language and content; promotes students' autonomy by (partly) making them responsible for their own learning through the collecting, assessing, and reporting of information gathered from target-language resources; involves (reflection on) both process and product; and extends over a longer period of time (weeks or months). We suggest that the main advantage of designing a Business English course around a particular project or set of projects (as we will illustrate on the basis of two case studies below) is that Business English learners can be exposed to – and learn to use – business language and business knowledge in order to communicate in business-relevant situations, using a variety of genres, channels, and media to help realize a complex set of interrelated project activities that contribute towards achieving higher-order or project-specific goals. Another important advantage of particular relevance to our discussion on intertextuality as a characteristic of workplace communication is that project-based learning means that learners do tasks that are not isolated, one-off communication events, but form an interrelated, interdependent set, simulating the real-life contexts in which learners will eventually need to work. Therefore, project-based learning allows learners to experience to some extent what it feels like to be a business professional, and to develop the beginnings of their professional identity and skill set. It is also particularly useful for learners at advanced levels as it allows them to move beyond general language proficiency in order to work on their professional Business English communication skills.

To illustrate this approach, we highlight two accounts of courses in which project-based learning is applied. The first is Nickerson (2015), who describes a course on business communication taught to senior business majors enrolled in the College of Business at Zayed University in the United Arab Emirates (UAE). The students' first language is Arabic, but they are also proficient speakers of English, and the course aims primarily to prepare them to become part of the UAE's workforce, which is highly globalized and multicultural and serves multiple sectors (ranging from (semi-)government to business). The lingua franca most often used in UAE business contexts is English. By the time the students take the course, they have already completed a foundation course in which they have developed the required English proficiency (i.e. an IELTS score of at least 5.0, equivalent to a Central European Framework proficiency level of B2) and the general study skills they need, and they are in their final two years of study towards a Bachelor's degree. Nickerson describes how the content of the business communication course is organized around two central learning objectives: 1) language, and 2) global awareness. These course objectives are operationalized further in a five-part model, the CLASP model, made up of the following components:

1 *Cultural literacy*: knowledge of culture and how it affects communication in business settings.
2 *Language and genre*: understanding the variety of genres available in business settings and developing the ability to use them to communicate strategically, including choice of channels, media, tone, style, structure, and language.
3 *Audience awareness*: audience analysis and how this determines the form and content of communication.
4 *Social capital and sustainability*: developing the ability to network, create goodwill, and establish and maintain positive relationships in business settings.
5 *Persuasion*: developing the ability to communicate effectively and reach desired goals.

(Nickerson, 2015, p. 7, slightly adapted)

The course runs for five months and is centred around five small-scale research projects on five selected topics, each of which is linked to a specific CLASP component. For example, while one project focuses on website communication (linked to the CLASP component 3, audience awareness), another centres on women and leadership communication (linked to CLASP component 5, persuasion). Each project ends with a research report and a project presentation in English, through which students work on their speaking and writing skills. The specialist content for the projects is provided through background readings, including journal articles and newspaper reports. A project typically starts with a series of exercises or "prompts" (Nickerson, 2015, p. 11) to sensitize students to the particular focus of the project and introduce them to the subsequent research required. These prompts form the basis for class discussion aimed at raising students' awareness of the specific topic. This awareness-raising is reinforced by their reading and subsequent discussion of the background literature. For example, for the project on English as an international language, Nickerson describes how students first consider a collection of authentic product advertisements used in the UAE in Arabic only, in English only, in a mix of English and Arabic, and in Anglicized Arabic. They are then asked to study a set of background readings on international advertising and language choice in advertising, and to consider – for discussion – questions such as: 1) How widespread is the use of English in the UAE? 2) What are consumers' attitudes to the use of English in advertising? and 3) Do they understand it in TV and print advertising? (Nickerson, 2015, p. 12).

By working on the five research projects, students develop and build not only their Business English and communication skills, but also more general, no less important, workplace skills such as time management, relationship-building, and collaboration, and also academic skills such as searching for, selecting, analyzing, and reporting information. Nickerson notes that within the course, English is effectively regarded and used as a conduit through which students apply and develop a broad skill set to achieve their project goals (Nickerson, 2015, p. 14). She also observes that the course allows her students to interact with their own community in a way that non-Emirati researchers could never hope to achieve (p. 13), providing invaluable and authentic input and interaction within the context of each of the projects.

The second example of project-based learning applied in a Business English course is provided by Planken et al. (2004), who describe the business language projects that form the basis of a Business English (or French, Spanish, or German) course for Dutch Bachelor degree students studying International Business Communication in their first year at university. For these students, English is a second language learned in a formal environment (secondary school), and their proficiency level in general English can be considered to be functional (IELTS at least 5.0, level B2 in terms of the Central European Framework) when they start the course. As in the UAE-based business communication course described above, a primary learning objective of the course is to develop students' proficiency in using English effectively for specific business purposes, and in a variety of business contexts. During the first two terms, the Business English course is supported with a language skills workshop that deals with the mechanics of English (grammar, business vocabulary, pronunciation, business writing conventions, etc.). Importantly, the course is also interdisciplinary: it connects with parallel core content courses in the rest of the Business Communication programme such as marketing, management and intercultural communication, in that content from those courses forms a substantial part of the business-related input for the four business language projects (one project per term) that students work on in their first year. We will refer primarily to one of the projects, which requires students, as a team and in the professional role of marketing consultants, to investigate the potential of the UK market, supposedly for a real Dutch company that wants to launch its products in the UK.

During the project, students complete a number of central learning tasks. They gather information about an existing (real) Dutch company, explore the target market (social and political factors and demography) and potential competitors in that market, and design a marketing survey to gauge UK consumers' interest in the product that the Dutch company aims to launch. To achieve these tasks, they use Business English in a number of business genres and settings. For example, they hold team meetings and give presentations about their progress, write business letters and emails to request information, report on information they have gathered online and through social media, design a questionnaire or interview scheme as part of the marketing survey, and write an interim and final recommendation report for the client company. Also, throughout the course, focused classroom activities reinforce these central awareness-raising and production tasks. In a similar way, as part of another business language project (exploring a cross-national joint venture), for instance, students are shown a video of a joint venture negotiation involving people with different nationalities using English as a Lingua Franca. They are asked to reflect on how different communicative functions such as proposal, acceptance/rejection, greeting, interruption, etc. are realized in English and by participants with different cultural backgrounds, and how participants in the negotiation respond to such communication. This type of activity is meant to sensitize learners not only to the linguistic repertoire required for negotiating in Business English as a Lingua Franca, but also to any cultural characteristics that may play a role in intercultural interactions (Planken et al., 2004).

Project-based learning can be particularly useful for mixed ability classes where learners have different levels of language proficiency, and for classes with advanced or near-native proficiency. This is because it allows individuals to contribute to a project in many different ways, and it does not just focus on language proficiency. Our own experience in developing and teaching the projects we have described in this section – in very different places and with very different students – would suggest that the most effective contributors within a project-based learning environment are not always those learners with the best English. Understanding the different roles that are needed in order to complete a project can often lead to a positive learning experience for everyone involved, while at the same time underlining how Business English combines with other necessary skills in the workplace. Using a project-based learning approach can be messy in the classroom compared to a traditional approach, and it requires flexibility on the part of the teacher. Students are generally much more actively involved, however, and therefore willing to invest their time in the learning process both inside and outside the classroom.

Another approach to teaching that is also centred around problem-solving and learning by doing is the Case Study Method. In Task 11.1, we ask you to consider this approach for your own teaching. The Case Study Method originated as a teaching approach at Harvard Business School and is often used in business schools around the world. In the Case Study Method, "Students are presented with the record of a problematic business situation that an organization has actually faced. They then have to reflect, interact, take responsibility, solve problems, and determine possible courses of action and their consequences" (Esteban & Pérez Cañado, 2004, p. 138). The Case Study Method requires students to produce language spontaneously and to complete a set of complex communication tasks. It can therefore be particularly useful for non-native learners of Business English at higher levels of proficiency, and for mixed ability groups ranging from those with functional language skills through to near-native competence.

Task 11.1 Using the Case Study Method

Read Esteban and Pérez Cañado's (2004) account of how the Case Study Method can be usefully incorporated into the Business English classroom, together with the advice given by Schullery (1999) on how to select an

)priate case. Make a list of the advantages and disadvantages of using this
.......od that these authors identify, together with the solutions they provide
for making it work.

Decide whether you could use this approach in your own teaching. What
type of case study would you use? What language would you focus on?

Esteban, A., & Pérez Cañado, M. (2004). Making the case method work in
teaching Business English: A case study. *English for Specific Purposes, 23,* 137–61.

Schullery, N. (1999). Selecting workable cases for classroom use. *Business
Communication Quarterly 62,* 77–80.

Team-teaching

A team-teaching approach to English for Specific Purposes means that English
language teachers team up with teachers in other relevant disciplines, that is,
with subject specialists, to inform their course design and in some cases to
actually teach the course. Primarily, then, the idea of team-teaching involves
the establishment of interdisciplinary partnerships. Dudley-Evans (2001, as
cited in Northcott & Brown, 2006) categorizes such partnerships, in the English
for Specific Purposes context, into three areas, depending on the level of
involvement: 1) cooperation, where the language teacher merely consults the
subject specialist about the specific discipline, 2) collaboration, where both
collaborate to develop course materials outside the classroom, and 3) team-
teaching, where both work together in the same classroom. The business language
projects described by Planken et al. (2004), for instance, which we discussed in
the previous section as an example of a project-based approach, involved some
degree of interdisciplinary partnership (at the first level of cooperation), in that
the Business English teachers consulted the marketing, management, and
intercultural communication specialists about their parallel course content,
after which they developed specific projects and learning tasks in which the
specialist and language content were integrated. Even at this level of interdisciplinary cooperation, the additional information contributed to the successful
development and execution of the course.

In an account of the development and implementation of a legal English
course for translators of European Union legal documents, Northcott and
Brown (2006) describe the relatively high degree of interdisciplinary cooperation
that occurred between law lecturers, teachers of English for Legal Purposes,
and legal translators in the design and teaching of a specialist translation
course for non-legally qualified legislative translators whose first language was
Estonian. This teaching approach combined collaboration outside the classroom and team-teaching within it in a complex interdisciplinary partnership.
Using an ethnographic approach – that is, by observing the course developers

and analyzing excerpts from video recordings of actual training sessions – they describe the process of course development in general and how the team-teaching approach in particular contributed to course design as well as to meeting the participants' needs. All participants in the specialist course were involved at the time in the translation of Estonian legislation into English, and European Union legislation into their first language. A needs analysis conducted prior to the course showed that participants not only wanted to improve their legal English, but also wanted to develop their knowledge of European Union law and common law systems, and to learn how to solve common terminology and translation problems. Following this, key legal topics were identified in areas in which the course participants were doing translation work. Next, in collaboration with the law lecturers and legal translators, the English for Legal Purposes teachers developed an approach to training which involved a sequence of paired lectures consisting of 1) legal concept seminars led by the legal specialists (providing law input on each of the specific legal topics iden-tified in the needs analysis), and 2) language review sessions led by the English for Legal Purposes teachers, based on their observations and the notes they took during the legal concept seminars. In each of the review sessions, the focus was on specific vocabulary and terminology that came up in the legal concept seminars, and the aim of the sessions was to clarify misunderstandings that arose in those seminars.

Based on their analysis of video excerpts from the training sessions, Northcott and Brown subsequently perceived a number of benefits of the team-teaching approach. They note, for example, that the acquisition of specialist terminology seems to have been considerably aided by the way in which the language review sessions allowed discussion of the law input, and specifically the legal concepts and terminology associated with the different legal topics, from both a linguistic and a legal perspective. Also, the interdisciplinary nature of the sessions encouraged participants to discuss translation problems from their own as well as from another person's perspective, which gave them valuable insights into each other's frame of reference and facilitated collaborative solutions to translation problems. The sessions also encouraged participants to exchange knowledge based on experience in previous translation work to allow them to identify each other's best practices. Northcott and Brown conclude that it is important for translators to "understand legal methods and knowing how to think like lawyers and ask legal questions" (2006, p. 374). To create a learning environment in which this type of process is possible, the inter-disciplinary input that can be achieved through team-teaching would seem to be indispensable.

Collaboration at any of the three levels of interdisciplinary partnership that Dudley-Evans suggests is a useful way for Business English teachers to create a meaningful classroom experience if they do not have a business background. This can range from identifying appropriate topics to be discussed in class or incorporated into a project, as Planken at el. (2004) describe, through to the complex collaborative work on the communication skills needed for translators, discussed by Northcott and Brown (2006).

In the next chapter, we look in more detail at the development of teaching materials for use in the Business English classroom and discuss ways in which teachers can collect the information that they need in order to do this.

Task 11.2 Incorporating a team-teaching approach

Over the past decade, Samantha Sin, an accountancy professor, and Alan Jones, an applied linguist, have collaborated together on understanding more about the English communication skills that accountants in Australia need. Their students are a mix of Australian and international students, so members of the teaching team have needed to develop appropriate materials for varying levels of language proficiency. In order to do this, they have combined survey research and a genre approach to generate a useful set of teaching materials, and they have then incorporated team-teaching into the classroom and a joint evaluation process into the way in which their students are assessed (Sin et al., 2007; Sin, 2011; Sin et al., 2012).

Consider the design of a course for a specific group of Business English users (e.g. accountants, translators, land surveyors, etc.) in the country where you are teaching, and decide how you could incorporate a team-teaching approach into that course. Think about the different levels of interdisciplinary partnership that you would need in order to do this, together with the information that you would need to collect.

Blended learning

The third English for Special Purposes approach that can be usefully incorporated into Business English courses is blended learning, an approach in which traditional learning (i.e. face-to-face language classes) is combined with ICT (information and communications technology)-supported and/or online learning methods. Since the publication of the pioneering work by Brett (2000), which deals with how to integrate multimedia specifically into the Business English classroom, the incorporation of ICT-based learning methods in language-learning courses has become increasingly popular. At the same time, younger learners have been adopting ICT-based applications to communicate with one another and to gain access to information in their everyday lives. The assumption of course designers has generally been that learners will therefore react positively to ICT-based methods, and that their incorporation in language courses will increase learners' engagement and aid the learning process. Rapanta et al. (2014) provide an account of a project-based "mobile learning initiative" (p. 358) taught in the final year of an otherwise traditional business communication course for undergraduate business students at Zayed University in the United Arab Emirates. This course, on business communication, also featured in the first account of project-based learning that we discussed earlier (Nickerson, 2015).

The mobile learning initiative required students to create chapters of an iBook relating to three of the five special topics, or modules, in the course, namely: 1) intercultural communication, 2) website communication, and 3) communication on corporate social responsibility. The blended approach was seen as particularly relevant to business students, for whom ICT skills are also an important pedagogical objective. We discussed a similar approach in Chapter 8 when we showed how Gimenez (2014) had incorporated computer-mediated communication into a set of classroom simulations. In addition, in the UAE and elsewhere, locally produced teaching materials of relevance for senior business students are limited, and this prompted Rapanta et al. to work with their students to develop course content on each of the selected topics that would appeal to their specific target group and fulfil their specific business communication needs. Students were provided with iPads and divided into groups representing courseware developers and peer assessors. One group of male students acted as courseware developers and two groups of female students acted as peer assessors, so that the two genders could take part in the same project but still remain segregated, as is the norm in federal universities in the UAE. The developers were given a short course on using the Apple application Creative Book Builder, with which teaching materials can be created for use with an iPad. Students were required to design a "final product [in English] that looked like a professional handbook that could be of use to people interested in doing business [in the Middle East]" (Rapanta et al., 2014, p. 363).

Rapanta et al. describe an example of one of the students' final products. The iBook module designed to accompany the topic Intercultural Communication, for example, consisted of a video on intercultural communication (drawn from the internet), a cartoon on communication between national and expatriate employees (made by the students), and a case study on cultural differences between the UAE and another country (based on information from the internet). It also featured a journalist's video report about a neighbouring country (taken from the internet), and an interactive quiz (made by the students) to test readers' knowledge of the skills needed to be an effective manager in the context of the UAE (Rapanta et al., 2014, p. 365). Through surveys and focus-group discussions with the students, Rapanta et al. also investigated how responsive students were to the mobile learning initiative. The students were motivated by the initiative as part of the overall, project-based course, and regarded the iPad-based activities in general, and the integration of video content in particular, as interesting. The initiative was also received positively by many of the students because it involved teamwork and collaboration, which reflected the fact that Emirati culture tends to be very group oriented.

Conversely, some students reported that they missed the student-teacher interaction, suggesting that relying on ICT-based learning only may be disadvantageous. Rapanta et al. concluded that the "cultural immediacy" of the topics discussed increased the emotional involvement of the students, and it was likely that this would have contributed to a positive learning environment (2014, p. 371).

Task 11.3 Reflecting on different approaches to teaching

Think of a course in English you have either taken yourself or were asked to develop and teach. Did any of the English for Specific Purposes approaches that we have discussed in this chapter – i.e. project-based learning, team-teaching or blended learning – feature in the course?

If 'yes', then how was the approach used in the course? Do you think that the approach worked? Did it contribute to the learning process?
If 'no', then how might these approaches have been incorporated, on their own or in combination? What could they have achieved? Refer back to the various projects we have referred to in this chapter to help you.

Summary

The teaching approaches that we have discussed in this chapter can provide added value to Business English courses in different ways, both in terms of the different skill sets they can help to develop, and in the variety of teaching contexts in which they can be successfully used. Firstly, each approach enables students to develop and build their business language and business communication skill set, as well as the other skills that are required in a workplace setting such as time and project management, effective multi-communication, problem-solving, decision-making, investigating skills, and (crosscultural) collaboration. Project-based learning would seem to be particularly useful in this regard as it requires students to work on a complex, relatively large-scale, overarching assignment (the project), for which they need to carry out a set of interrelated tasks, over a period of time, to achieve the assignment's (learning) objectives. Secondly, each approach provides course designers with the opportunity to integrate and present authentic, specialist (i.e. business-related) content as input for communication-centred activities and language-centred tasks. Authentic, content-based input can help to make business language more meaningful to learners because it presents the language in a context of use that is directly relevant to them. This, in turn, can enhance language learning as well as learners' performance in more general areas such as problem-solving, analyzing, and reporting. Finally, the adoption of any of these approaches by a Business English course, on its own or in combination, is likely to contribute to the creation of a learning environment that is more realistic for students, in that it will reflect more closely the conditions that govern the (communicative) activities students will eventually be asked to undertake in the workplace, as business professionals, and in English.

In the next chapter, we discuss the different approaches that English for Specific Purposes scholars and practitioners have taken to the development of course materials for the teaching of Business English. We include a more detailed discussion on how to conduct a needs analysis survey or a communication audit, and how to use this information in course design, and we also show how needs analysis can be combined with corpus analysis to develop a specific set of teaching materials.

Chapter 12

Designing Business English Teaching Materials

Introduction

Throughout this volume, we have emphasized the importance of accommodating Business English learners' specific workplace needs in course design, and of using authentic spoken and written Business English as a basis for developing Business English course materials. We have also highlighted, in agreement with many of the researchers whose studies we discussed in our previous chapters, that tasks and assignments for the Business English classroom should expose learners to complex rather than single tasks which involve authentic business content and a variety of different business genres (e.g. email, meeting, report, negotiation, presentation, etc.). They should also aim to simulate real business situations (e.g. a sales negotiation, a joint merger meeting, a job interview, etc.) and to recreate real workplace contexts (e.g. internal, external, international, multilingual, etc.). Furthermore, we have suggested that classroom tasks and materials should be designed to promote learners' awareness of the characteristics of everyday communication in the workplace, such as the reliance on intertextuality and multimodality; and we have recommended that they should incorporate the complete skill set required to function effectively in the workplace using Business English, including being able to build business relationships (across cultures), to multi-communicate, and to be fluent not only in traditional but also in emerging genres and media (i.e. to master multimedia literacy). Only if we create courses and materials that reflect real-life business conditions and encourage learners to actively use Business English in business-relevant situations can we begin to offer a learning environment in the Business English classroom that mirrors the communication situations in which students of Business English will ultimately find themselves. Creating such an environment offers learners the relevant input they need – in terms of business and language knowledge, skills training, and awareness-raising – to develop truly 'functional competence' in Business English, which means that they have the language and communication proficiency they need to function like a native speaker in professional and business contexts (cf. Kachru's "functional nativeness", 2005, discussed in Nickerson, 2015).

In this chapter, we look at the design of teaching materials for different groups of Business English learners. We discuss the different approaches that English for Specific Purposes researchers and practitioners have taken in developing materials, and we show how this information has been used both in the design of specific tasks for a particular group of students and in the construction of textbooks. In the final section of the chapter, we consider assessment and how to approach this for Business English.

English for Specific Purposes researchers and practitioners have taken three main approaches to the development of materials for Business English: a needs analysis survey or communication audit carried out within a specific profession or organization; a corpus-based study of the language or genres that specific groups of Business English learners will need to use; and a survey of existing textbook materials with a focus on a specific business genre or a specific language strategy. We will discuss each of these approaches in turn and show how these have been used to generate a new set of materials or a new set of tasks.

Textbox 12.1 Curriculum design in mainland China

Zhang (2007) is a review of the changes that have taken place in teaching Business English in mainland China from the middle of the twentieth century onwards, including how these changes have impacted curriculum design. Zhang shows that the most recent approaches are now research-based, incorporating ideas from both English for Specific Purposes and business discourse studies. This allows him to propose the following working definition of Business English and what it means to teach Business English:

> Business English involves the teaching of the system of strategic communication in the social and economic domain of international business in which participants, adopting/adapting business conventions and procedures, make selective use of lexicogrammatical resources of English as well as visual and audio semiotic resources to achieve their communicative goals via the writing modality, speaking modality, and/or multimodality.
>
> (Zhang, 2007, p. 406)

Following on from this definition, Zhang draws on Bhatia (2002) and proposes a tripartite curriculum for teaching Business English consisting of business studies (disciplinary knowledge), business discourse (discursive competence), and business practice (professional practice). Business discourse consists of the skills needed for study (e.g. presentations and discussions) together with the genres needed for work (e.g. meetings, negotiations, correspondence etc.).

Zhang also suggests a set of awareness-raising activities focusing on language, such as improving language accuracy and learning to use a genre appropriately. Language skills are therefore seen as an integral part of business expertise and are taught in an integrated way, rather than being treated as a discrete subject area.

Needs analysis surveys and communication audits

Business English is taught both at university level, where it tends to be a specific type of Business English related to an academic discipline, and in post-experience courses, where it is often taught with an emphasis on general business language skills rather than being associated with a particular profession. While some Business English practitioners have carried out a communication audit in order to develop materials for post-experience professionals, the scholarly work on Business English that takes an English for Specific Purposes approach has been dominated by the identification of student learner needs, often involving what is referred to as a needs analysis survey. In their extensive account of needs analysis for language course design within the Common European Framework Professional Profiles Project, Huhta et al. (2013) draw on Brown's (2006) work, and provide the following description of what it means to carry out a needs analysis:

> Needs analysis is the systematic collection and analysis of all subjective and objective information necessary to define and validate defensible curriculum purposes that satisfy the language learning requirements of students within the context of the particular institutions that influence the learning and teaching situation.
>
> (Brown, 2006, p. 102)

In Huhta et al.'s (2013) account, this means understanding the language needs relating to the profession, the occupation, and the specific context that an individual belongs to, as well as knowing about the situations in which the target language is used, both in routine and more challenging situations. Further information is provided by Flowerdew (2013), in her comprehensive overview of needs analysis and the development of different curricula in the teaching of English for Specific Purposes. She also underlines the fact that needs analysis has been applied to English for Academic Purposes more often than to English for Occupational Purposes or Business English. This means that English for Academic Business Purposes has been investigated much more often than English for Professional Business Purposes.

Teaching practitioners usually carry out a needs analysis on the basis of a survey designed to find out what a professional community or discipline needs to do with Business English. They ask a set of questions on topics such as when the specific community needs English, what they need to write (or speak), who they need to communicate with, and, crucially, if there are activities that they do not engage in because of a lack of language skills. Questions like these allow teaching practitioners to identify the genres that they need to incorporate into their course, and to pinpoint any skills that their students potentially need to complete additional tasks through the medium of Business English and perhaps to further their careers.

There are numerous examples of needs analysis surveys carried out by English for Specific Purposes researchers with an interest in discipline-specific Business English targeted at tertiary level learners. These range from large-scale to small-scale studies. An example of a large-scale study is the multi-layered project carried out in Hong Kong to identify the Business English needs of students following tertiary level business education. The project considers six different perspectives: a student perspective, a teacher perspective, a curriculum perspective, a writing performance perspective, a textual perspective, and an occupational perspective (described in Jackson, 2005, and Bargiela-Chiappini et al., 2013). An example of a needs analysis on a smaller scale is the genre-based account given by Evans (2012), which we described in detail in Chapter 8 and which specifically identified the email tasks that business professionals need in key industries in Hong Kong. Other studies, such as Fuertes-Olivera and Gómez-Martínez (2004) in Spain and Trinder (2013) in Austria, use student perceptions of their learning process and an analysis of various learning factors in a different form of needs analysis. They do so in order to make recommendations on the content of Business English courses, with a focus on how to create an effective learning experience. Later in this chapter, we consider several studies that have combined a needs analysis survey with an analysis of the genres and language that a professional or disciplinary group uses.

In post-experience courses outside tertiary education, Business English practitioners may carry out a communication audit in order to select appropriate tasks and materials for their learners. This is similar to a needs analysis and often also takes the form of a survey, but it aims to identify any problems within a specific corporate setting in both communication and language use (Charles & Marschan-Piekkari, 2002). A communication audit tries to establish the situations and genres that require a foreign language (e.g. Business English), and those that require the use of the local language. In doing so, it also emphasizes the gap between the skills that already exist within a corporation and those that are still required. In Chapter 2, we discussed the study of horizontal communication at the multinational corporation Kone Elevators carried out by Charles and Marschan-Piekkari (2002). This took the form of a communication audit. In their account, the authors comment that an effective audit can be used to identify "(a) the situations in which staff engage (or would engage, if language skills existed) in communication, (b) the people between whom communication takes place (or would take place, if language skills existed), and (c) the language(s) currently used" (Charles & Marschan-Piekkari, 2002, p. 24).

In addition to the account given by Charles and Marschan-Piekkari (2002), we have discussed several studies that used a communication audit as the basis for a set of training materials. For example, Lockwood (2012), whose study was discussed in Chapter 1, created a set of materials specifically designed for call centre employees after she had spent some time talking to them and finding out what tasks they needed to achieve through Business English. Baxter et al. (2002), featured in Chapter 7, used a communication audit at the Hong Kong Jockey Club involving questionnaires and interviews to help the research team to plan a set of activities centred on the genre of the committee paper. Other accounts that rely on a communication audit include Nickerson (2009), who used interviews and several focus group discussions to advise on the components of a Business English course for the call centre software engineers at a major multinational corporation based in India. Randall and Samimi (2010) discuss an audit carried out at the Dubai Police Force in the UAE that had a focus on when they needed English and what they needed it for. Kassim and Ali (2010) surveyed the engineers at ten multinational chemical companies across Malaysia and found that they needed the Business English speaking skills necessary to participate effectively in communicative events such as teleconferences, networking, and presenting new ideas and strategies. Finally, Sin (2011) reports on her interviews with accounting professionals in the Australian context and reveals that communicative expertise was considered as instrumental in maintaining trust in the interpersonal relationships that underpin many accounting and (most particularly) auditing activities, and that trust should therefore be a focus in Business English training (Jones & Sin, 2012; Sin 2011).

All of these studies share a concern with how business professionals communicate through Business English and how it is used to achieve their work-related tasks. While the information a communication audit provides can clearly be used to help in designing an appropriate set of tasks for business people who do not speak or write English as their first language, it can also be used to design materials for mixed proficiency classes such as those we discussed in the previous chapter, and for situations in which first and foreign language users of Business English work alongside each other.

Task 12.1 Using a communication audit

Review the descriptions of Lockwood (2012) in Chapter 1, Charles and Marschan-Piekkari (2002) in Chapter 2, and Baxter et al. (2002) in Chapter 7. In each case, decide how the researchers collected the data they needed to design a set of appropriate training materials for the situation in which they were working.

Think of a similar situation with which you are familiar and plan a communication audit that would allow you to collect the same type of information.
Who would you need to talk to?
What would you ask them?

Corpus-based approaches

In our discussion on spoken Business English in Part II of this book, we noted the importance of corpus-based studies as input for course development and teaching materials, not only because corpora can provide authentic language examples for course developers, but also because such studies have uncovered ways in which Business English differs from general English, or from English as it is used in domains other than business. In this section we profile two corpus-based studies that throw light on different aspects of Business English use and in doing so provide usable suggestions as to how such findings might be incorporated into Business English teaching materials. The first is by Koester (2014), whose work on Business English already featured at some length in Part II. In this 2014 account, she considers the use of a specific feature of Business English in negotiations, namely hypothetical reported speech (HRS); that is, reporting what a party or parties in a negotiation might, hypothetically speaking, say or do (e.g. "So, if you and me were to say that we cut these prices further ... "). Koester and Handford (2013) found that the use of hypothetical reported speech was frequent in negotiations and meetings involving negotiation, and that this was the case across different types of meetings and a variety of business sectors. Koester (2014) therefore wanted to examine the specific – functional – role of hypothetical reported speech in negotiations by looking at where it occurs, what functions it performs, and whether negotiators use it as a strategic tool (p. 36).

The corpus Koester examined consisted of four meetings involving "substantial negotiation activity" (p. 38) taken from the Cambridge and Nottingham Corpus of Business English (CANBEC). Koester identified negotiating sequences that contained HRS and subsequently analyzed these sequences at micro-level using conversation analysis techniques. HRS was found to occur in all of the meetings, most frequently in the bargaining phase of negotiation segments, and in "both the 'proposal' and 'response' moves" (Koester, 2014, p. 39). In other words, it occurred in offers and requests (proposals) and in explanations and refusals (responses). Koester shows how negotiators use HRS (presented in italics in the examples below, taken from her corpus) strategically. For instance, Koester describes how a negotiator uses HRS to encourage the other party to move closer towards a particular agreement (e.g. "You just have a look at it first and you come back and tell us *'Yep we can do that and we can do it to that price'*", Koester, 2014, p. 39, slightly adapted). Also, she shows how, as part of an explanation or so-called 'account', HRS is used to refuse a particular offer from the other party (e.g. "So this would be double work for us to say '*Okay we have to cancel one order and increase the next order.*' Because they are on a different time line", Koester, 2014, p. 39, slightly adapted). Koester suggests that in the latter example, the use of HRS allows the speaker to soften a potentially face-threatening act (e.g. of rejecting the other party's suggestion or offer). It is softened in the sense that the refusal to comply, and the reasoning underlying it, is not made explicit but is only indirectly referred to. HRS is also used as a strategy to construct the negotiators' working relationship. Negotiators show, for example, that they are prepared to improve an offer in favour of the other party: "But obviously we can look at compressing what you've got down into one rack, and then sort of saying, '*well obviously you can take half a rack if and when you need it*'" (Koester, 2014, p. 44, slightly adapted).

Koester concludes that HRS is indeed an integral part of negotiating, and that it is used strategically to move the negotiation in a particular direction, downtone potentially face-threatening moves (e.g. rejections, disagreements, and refusals), and show affiliation with the other party (i.e. to build the relationship). Given the relative frequency of HRS and the fact that it occurs in the most important − bargaining − phase of negotiations, she suggests that learners of Business English "would benefit from learning when and how to use it in negotiation" (Koester, 2014, p. 45). According to Koester, supplementing materials with information that shows how learners can use HRS to employ these functions more strategically (e.g. more politely and persuasively) could greatly improve their overall performance in negotiation tasks, and would, above all, mirror real negotiation more closely. Furthermore, recordings or transcripts of authentic negotiations − or excerpts from negotiations − could be used to raise learners' awareness of the use of HRS, and to "focus their attention on the strategic functions that HRS [...] is used for in negotiating" (Koester, 2014, p. 45). A similar approach is in fact used in the corpus-based Business English coursebook developed by Koester and colleagues which we referred to in Part II, and which offers scripts based on authentic negotiating data from the CANBEC corpus (Koester et al., 2012). Finally, Koester recommends that learners be encouraged to develop a greater awareness of the importance of the relational dimension of negotiations. For example, the differences in the use of HRS in the four meetings could be explained by the nature of the relationship between the negotiators (new or old). Koester suggests that making learners aware of such links − between contextual factors and language use − is essential if they are to improve their performance in Business English, and to prepare them for real-life negotiation encounters.

In a similar way, Walker (2011) deftly demonstrates how corpus-based analysis can be particularly useful to the teaching of Business English in two ways: first, it can be used to highlight aspects of lexis − i.e. vocabulary and collocations (words that occur together with the target word) used in Business

English versus general English, and second, it can be used to provide answers to students' questions about collocations in a more accurate and specific way. In his account, Walker takes us through two case questions from students of Business English in relation to a specific set of lexical items and their collocations. The first case question is from a senior manager in a German company who is concerned about a presentation he has to give, and in particular about hitting the 'right tone' (he does not want to come across as authoritarian). The specific question is: "should I say I *run, manage,* or *head* the Human Resources Division, or should I use a phrase like I am *responsible for,* or *in charge of* instead?" (Walker, 2011, p. 104). What Walker shows us, step by step, is how frequency and concordance analyses in two corpora – the Bank of English corpus (BoE) and a corpus of business English drawn from the British National Corpus (BNC), (see also Part II) – can provide a well-reasoned answer to the question that is based on a systematic consideration of authentic language use.

By first deriving the most frequent collocations for *RUN, MANAGE* and *HEAD* in the BoE corpus, Walker demonstrates that *RUN* occurs more frequently in combination with *BUSINESS* than both *MANAGE* and *HEAD*. While *MANAGE* is frequently associated with financial items, including *MONEY, INVESTMENT,* etc., *HEAD* is mostly used with items referring to organizations or entities involving people, such as *TEAM, COMMITTEE, CLUB, INVESTIGATION,* but also *BUSINESS*. A more detailed look at the wider contexts in which *RUN* occurs shows how it seems to be frequently associated with power; it often occurs together with *COUNTRY* or *GOVERNMENT* (Walker, 2011). With respect to the phrases *RESPONSIBLE FOR* and *IN CHARGE OF,* analyses of collocations in the two corpora show that both items are used to describe the responsibility that someone (e.g. a team manager) or something (e.g. a business unit) has for a specific function in an organization, while only *RESPONSIBLE FOR* has an additional meaning in that it describes how someone can be accountable – in a negative sense – for a particular event or development, e.g. a *DEATH, LOSS,* or *ATTACK* (Walker, 2011). Finally, an examination of the contexts in which *IN CHARGE OF* occurs shows that it is used mostly with non-human entities (e.g. *COUNTRY, OPERATIONS, INVESTIGATION,* etc.) rather than with people, with the exception of a *TEAM*. Again, based on the corpus data, *IN CHARGE OF,* like *RUN,* would seem to be associated with authority (Walker 2011).

Walker concludes, in answer to the student's question, that he should not use *RUN* or *IN CHARGE OF* as both are associated with power and the authoritarian management style he is trying to avoid in his presentation. In particular, he should avoid the use of *RUN,* because it tends to be used with inanimate objects, which might give his audience the impression that he sees them as "automatons who simply have to be told what to do" (Walker, 2011, p. 110). Walker recommends instead that the student uses *MANAGE* or *RESPONSIBLE FOR* (the Human Resources Department) to reflect an inclusive management style and a humane orientation. Neither of these items seems to be associated with authority, and both are more frequently associated with people than non-human objects (Walker 2011, p. 110). By taking us through a corpus analysis, Walker's account demonstrates how such an analysis can be a useful resource for teachers and students alike. An examination of its collocates can help to disambiguate various uses of a particular word and can identify slight but often crucial differences in meaning. As Walker notes, such information is also invaluable to developers of Business English course materials.

Surveys of published materials

Chan (2009) provides a framework for evaluating Business English materials that aims specifically to bridge the gap between the Business English used by business professionals and the Business English presented in textbooks. Chan notes that while existing checklists to assess Business English materials certainly provide a useful point of departure for teachers, what is really needed is a "more rigorous" set of evaluation criteria that includes a consideration of the "linguistic aspects of the materials", based on research findings demonstrating how language is used in specific target (business) contexts, in addition to assessing the "practical considerations such as cost and availability, [... and] the kind of learner [...] and the topic areas covered" (Chan, 2009, p. 126). The incorporation of linguistic criteria would provide the level of detail that is needed to allow teachers, even if they have little or no background in business, to evaluate Business English materials with regard to "suitability, authenticity and credibility" (p. 126), and to identify and address areas that existing materials do not yet cover.

The framework Chan presents involves a review of research findings on Business English pedagogy as well as on the discourse features of a particular topic. This review is then used to generate a two-part checklist which teachers can use to assess existing materials on the particular topic, and to identify gaps in the materials. In her account, Chan uses business meetings as an example topic to demonstrate how the framework can be used. The six steps that make up the framework take the Business English teacher from research to practice, as follows:

Step 1   Reviewing relevant research.
Step 2   Organizing findings.
Step 3   Developing checklists.
Step 4   Evaluating materials.
Step 5   Identifying gaps.
Step 6   Dealing with the gaps.

(Chan, 2009, p. 127)

Chan's account shows how her review of research (Steps 1 and 2 of the framework) uncovers a number of central themes. These relate, firstly, to the pedagogical considerations of teaching English for business meetings, and, secondly, to the specific characteristics of business meetings discourse. The pedagogical themes she identifies are "needs analysis, spoken grammar and authenticity, approach to teaching the language of meetings, and learner autonomy" (p. 128). With respect to spoken grammar and authenticity, for example, Chan finds that corpus-based research of spoken Business English has thrown light on the specific features of spoken Business English (versus spoken General English), as demonstrated in the work of Koester (2006) on spoken business genres, Nelson (2006) on Business versus General English, and Handford (2010) on meetings, all of which we discussed at some length in Part II of this book. For example, Koester's research shows how vague language is a common feature of spoken grammar in business contexts, and that it is used not only to tone down a speaker's direct statements (for example in the case of face-threatening speech acts) but also to reach interpersonal goals in interaction by promoting informality and intimacy (see also Part II). With respect to discourse features, Chan identifies five themes, namely "goal orientation, language used in meetings, strategies used in meetings, the structure of meetings, and cultural differences" (Chan, 2009, p. 129). For example, in relation to the theme cultural differences, Chan concludes on the basis of Rogerson-Revell's (2008) study (see also Part II) that there are differences not only in the discourse that people from different cultures produce in meetings, but also in the strategies they use to overcome additional communication problems when engaged in crosscultural meetings in which Business English as a Lingua Franca is used.

Based on the pedagogical and discoursal considerations that follow from the research review, Chan then generates a checklist (Step 3 of the framework: see Textbox 12.2 below), which she uses to evaluate 14 units on business meetings taken from eight mainstream Business English textbooks (Steps 4 and 5 of the framework). Finally, based on this evaluation, she identifies areas in which the existing materials lack information and examples and suggests how these gaps may be filled (Step 6 of the framework).

Textbox 12.2 A two-part checklist for evaluating business meeting materials

Part A: Pedagogical considerations (two of the six areas identified by Chan are given here)

Needs analysis. Does the material suit the learners' needs with regard to work experience and the types of meeting they will be involved in? Is the content relevant to business? Does it draw on the professional business people's meeting experiences? Are the activities and tasks suitable for the course's target group (i.e. their level and interest)?

Naturalness of the language models. Are authentic materials or samples of authentic spoken language used? Does the material contain features of natural speech? Does the material cover the features of spoken grammar that are relevant to business meetings?

Part B: Meeting discourse features (two of the six areas identified by Chan are given here)

Cultural differences. Does the material sensitize learners to cultural differences in meeting styles? Do tasks and activities help learners to practise the skills and strategies required to effectively hold crosscultural meetings?
Strategies. Are learners equipped with strategies that will allow them to show both positive and negative politeness in meetings? Does the material offer the language to implement these strategies?

(Chan, 2009, p. 132, slightly adapted)

Overall, Chan concludes that while the business meetings materials she assessed all provide sufficient input for learners to practise speaking and listening skills related to meetings, the examples, language, and strategies offered in the materials are not always authentic, and are usually scripted. She recommends that teaching materials for business meetings should therefore be supplemented with authentic examples of 'meeting talk' from corpus-based studies in order to to reflect the language and strategies business professionals use in real-life meetings. What Chan's account shows is how a research-based checklist such as the one she generates for business meetings materials can be usefully employed to help Business English teachers in a number of ways. Firstly, it can help them to assess existing materials with respect to "effectiveness, suitability, and authenticity" (Chan, 2009, p. 134), as well as to identify areas that existing materials do not address. Secondly, it can provide them with suggestions as to how to fill such gaps. Finally, it can provide them with a basis for developing new materials.

In a similar way to Chan, Bremner (2008, 2010) provides two insightful accounts of coursebook analyses in which he assesses the extent to which teaching materials reflect actual workplace practice with respect to two areas that business communication research identifies as being essential to workplace writing: intertextuality (Bremner, 2008) and collaborative writing (Bremner, 2010). In Chapter 9 of the current volume we also considered how research has shown the importance of intertextuality to Business English in general. In his 2008 account, Bremner evaluates eight coursebooks on business communication on whether and how they deal with intertextuality in the context of business writing. For instance, he assesses the extent to which the coursebooks sensitize the learner to the intertextual nature of workplace writing, and the extent to which tasks and assignments reflect intertextuality – for example by highlighting how the text planning phase often relies on pre-existing texts produced elsewhere in the workplace. In other words, intertextuality can be signalled by highlighting how a text that is under construction is interlinked with, and based on, other texts. Bremner's analysis also considers whether the coursebooks feature collaborative writing, which research has shown to be a common feature of intertextuality in workplace communication (for more detail on Bremner's evaluation of collaborative writing as a feature of workplace writing materials, see his 2010 account).

Overall, the findings Bremner (2008) reports demonstrate that while the coursebooks do provide practice tasks which present background information aimed at helping the learner write a text, this information is never presented in the form of related texts that the learner can refer to in doing the task, but is instead presented in the form of a scripted context telling the learner what happened before (a case description) and what needs to be done (the brief). In other words, although the scripted context may refer to other texts, the actual texts referred to are never provided as input for the writing tasks. Based on this analysis, Bremner concludes therefore that intertextuality as a feature of workplace writing remains largely implicit in coursebooks, noting that the term intertextuality was in fact never used in any of the books he investigated. He recommends that textbooks on workplace writing, and on business communication in general, should more clearly reflect the fact that "workplace texts are interlinked with and shaped by other texts" (Bremner, 2008, p. 315). This could be done by incorporating examples of pre-existing texts in task descriptions, and by (at the very least) describing the links between pre-existing texts and the new text to be produced as the output of the task. This would not only create more authentic writing contexts, but also more realistic writing tasks.

The final survey of teaching materials we discuss in this chapter is Lam et al.'s (2014) evaluation of the teaching resources used in an elective Business English module that is taught as part of the English language curriculum at the City University of Hong Kong. Lam et al.'s analysis set out to determine what spoken and written business genres featured most frequently in the teaching and learning resources, and to what extent the focus in course materials reflected the use of such genres in actual professional settings in Hong Kong. The researchers also investigated how the most frequently featured spoken and written professional genres were presented (for example in terms of examples and linguistic realizations) in the course materials, and how these representations compared to the actual examples of these genres in the Hong Kong workplace. Their analysis showed that the most frequent (top five) spoken professional genres that featured in the course materials were business phone calls, handling complaints, business meetings, business presentations, and making complaints (Lam et al., 2014, p. 72). By comparison, Evan's (2010) survey of actual professional genre use in the Hong Kong workplace, which Lam et al. used as a baseline for their research, showed that the most frequent (top five) professional genres in real life were formal meetings, conferences, seminars, presentations, and telephone calls. With respect to written professional genres, Lam et al. found that the top five in the course materials were email messages, reports, letters, memos, and faxes/legal documents (Lam et al., 2014, p. 73). In contrast, Evans' survey found that the top five written genres in the workplace were handling complaints, business emails, business letters, business memos, and making complaints (Evans, 2010). In other words, while the module's course materials reflected the reality of the Hong Kong workplace to some extent, the relationship between pedagogy and reality was by no means one to one, as some of the genres used most frequently in the Hong Kong workplace (i.e. handling and making complaints, and conferences and seminars) did not feature in the top five genres featured in the course materials.

The most prominent finding from Lam et al.'s analysis, however, related to the way in which the professional genres were represented in the course materials. Language examples were for the large part presented in a decontextualized vacuum. In other words, only minimal information was given on the way in which contextual factors such as industry sector, type of organization, culture, power differences, social distance, individual interests, etc. influence the language used to realize a particular genre. We saw in Chapter 5 that a number of other researchers have made similar observations about Business English coursebooks and teaching materials, suggesting that examples of Business English are rarely presented in context and are only infrequently accompanied by explanations of how that context shapes the language or discourse.

Overall, Lam et al.'s survey uncovered a number of discrepancies between what is dealt with and described in the course materials and what is actually observed in workplace contexts (as reported by Evans, 2010). They recommend that course materials in future draw on a greater variety of samples (produced in different workplace contexts) of a particular genre rather than just a generic, single example. They also recommend an inductive approach to learning in which students are encouraged to consider sets of real-life examples of a particular genre (perhaps taken from the internet or from academic studies on the genre) with respect to characteristics of the text or interaction such as structure, linguistic realizations, moves, etc., so that they "can draw their own conclusions regarding similarities and differences of specific genres in different workplace settings based on their [own] analysis of corpus data" (Lam et al., 2014, p. 76; and see also previously for corpus-based approaches to Business English). In addition, Lam et al. recommend that samples of language use in the workplace that are featured in course materials should be presented in context; that is, together with information on the way in which contextual factors can influence not only the linguistic realization of genres (and the moves within those genres), but also the frequency and use of different professional genres, which research shows us can vary across industries, companies, and even business units within a company.

Task 12.2 Developing classroom activities

The edited collection by Chan and Frendo (2014) entitled *New ways in teaching business English* contains 80 classroom activities for use in teaching Business English. These activities were provided by Business English practitioners who were working in tertiary education, corporate language training, and adult education in various parts of the world. The contributions range across a variety of different topics such as spoken and written business communication, working with authentic materials and language, and intercultural communication, and they include activities designed to underpin tasks in the classroom like creating a corporate profile, writing a request email, and telling a story to make a point at work. Each activity contains details on the language proficiency level that it could be used with, the context where it could be used, the aims of the activity, the preparation time required, the class time that it would take, and any additional resources. This is then followed by a short description of the activity.

Review the surveys of published materials that we have discussed in this chapter (Chan, 2009, Bremner, 2008, and Lam et al., 2014). Develop a classroom activity that you could use to teach a specific aspect of Business English with a focus on how real-life communication occurs in the context of a business organization. Make a list of what type of learners you would use this activity with, what you would be aiming for, and how long it would take, and then write a short description of how to carry out the activity in class.

Additional Resources: Chan, C., & E. Frendo (Eds.) (2014). *New ways in teaching business English*. Alexandria, VA: TESOL.

Assessment

The assessment of Business English does not seem to have been a major concern for researchers or practitioners in English for Specific Business Purposes. As noted by Douglas (2013), in his overview of English for Specific Purposes and assessment in general, the account given by O'Sullivan (2006) makes a major contribution to the discipline through its discussion of the testing of English for business purposes. In this account, O'Sullivan reviews a range of different tests that have been developed for the testing of Business English, including the theory behind each one, and puts forward the argument that "the construct of Business English is clearly definable but that work still needs to be done in the area of linking test tasks to language knowledge" (Douglas, 2013, p. 375). Outside this general account of assessment in Business English, other useful accounts in English for Specific Purposes are provided by individual scholars working in a specific context, such as Friginal (2013), who describes the development and use of an oral performance assessment instrument which aimed to evaluate

Filipino agents' customer service transactions with callers from the US (see also our discussion on Lockwood, 2012 in Chapter 1) and Zhang (2013), who investigated how business professionals assessed the texts written by Business English students (as we discussed in detail in Chapter 8). Finally, the associated field of business communication may also provide some insights into assessment that have relevance for the teaching of Business English, as exemplified by Fraser et al.'s (2005) account of writing assessment at a US university, and a similar account of the assessment of learning outcomes in business communication in the UAE provided by Nickerson and Goby (2014). What these studies all show is that meaningful assessment may take place in many different ways, depending on the specific context, and not just through the internationally recognized Business English language tests.

Summary

In this chapter, we have looked at the three main approaches that English for Specific Purposes researchers and practitioners have taken in developing materials and curricula for Business English: needs analysis or communication audits, corpus-based studies, and surveys of existing textbook materials. We have shown how the information gathered using each approach has then been used to identify the most appropriate tasks for a specific group of students as well as to construct training courses, textbook materials and, in one case, a national integrated curriculum. We have also considered assessment and how to approach this for Business English.

In the next, and final chapter in this volume, we provide a set of relevant additional reading materials, together with other resources such as conferences and professional societies concerned with researching and teaching Business English.

Chapter 13

Business English Resources

Books and textbooks

References for the sources discussed in this volume can be found at the end of the book. The following are additional book-length studies, edited collections, and recent journal special issues that are also worth consulting.

Bargiela-Chiappini, F. (Ed.) (2009). *Handbook of business discourse*. Edinburgh: Edinburgh University Press.

This is a comprehensive overview of current research in the field of business discourse. It includes a wide range of contributions from researchers located in different parts of the world and covers both different research approaches and different cultural perspectives.

Basturkmen, H. (2005). *Ideas and options in English for specific purposes*. Hillsdale, N.J.: Lawrence Erlbaum Associates.

This volume provides an extensive account of the link between theory and the most important approaches that have been taken in teaching and research in English for Specific Purposes. It includes a section on English for Professional Purposes as well as one on English for Vocational Purposes.

Bhatia, V. K. (1993). *Analysing genre. Language use in professional settings*. London: Longman.

This is the seminal volume in which Bhatia introduces his ideas on genre, with particular reference to professional communication. It includes material on how to analyze written business genres such as application letters and sales letters using a moves analysis.

Nickerson, C. (Ed.) (2005). Special issue on English as a lingua franca in business contexts. *English for Specific Purposes Journal*, 24(4), 367–452.

This special issue provides an overview of work on Business English as a Lingua Franca in various geographical locations. It includes Louhiala-Salminen et al.'s (2005) defining article on BELF as well as specific analyses of negotiations, how English is used in the banking industry in Hong Kong and an account of teaching English for the global workplace in tertiary business education.

Orr, T. (Ed.) (2002). *English for specific purposes*. Alexandria, VA: TESOL, Inc.
This edited collection is a set of 12 case studies that look at different aspects of
   English for Specific Purposes. The first part deals with language learners in
   university settings and the second with language learners in the workplace. It
   includes the account given by Baxter et al. (2002) of their development of a
   training programme for the Hong Kong Jockey Club.
Orr, T. (Ed.) (2006). Special issue on insights from corpus linguistics
   for professional communication. *IEEE Transactions on Professional
   Communication, 49*(3).
This special issue looks at the contribution that corpus linguistics can make to
   understanding more about professional communication. The articles include
   an account of how a corpus approach can be used in the Business English
   classroom, as well as corpus-based analyses of annual general reports and
   the letters that appear in textbooks.
Paltridge, B. & Starfield, S. (Eds.) (2012). *Handbook of English for specific
   purposes*. Malden, MA: Wiley-Blackwell.
This volume provides an extensive survey of research in the field of English for
   Specific Purposes, including research methods and research-based teaching
   practices. It includes several contributions of relevance for research and
   teaching Business English on topics such as English in the workplace, English
   as a Lingua Franca, and Business English.

Journals

This is a list of journals that have featured contributions on researching or
teaching Business English, or on English for Specific Purposes more generally
(i.e. English for different professions).

Annual Review of Applied Linguistics (ARAL, Cambridge University Press)
English for Specific Purposes (Elsevier)
English Today (Cambridge University Press)
IEEE Transactions on Professional Communication (IEEE)
International Review of Applied Linguistics in Language Teaching (Walter de
   Gruyter)
Journal of Applied Linguistics (JAL, Equinox)
Language Teaching (Cambridge University Press)
TESOL Quarterly (TESOL International Association)
World Englishes (Blackwell Publishing)

Professional associations

The following associations and professional organizations hold conferences on
a regular basis which could be relevant for teachers and researchers of Business
English (see also below).

Association Internationale de Linguistique Appliquée. (International Association of Applied Linguistics) AILA:

http://www.aila.info

British Association of Applied Linguistics (BAAL):

http://www.aila.info/about/index.html

International Association for Teaching English as a Foreign Language (IATEFL):

http://www.iatefl.org

Teaching English to Speakers of Other Language (TESOL):

http://www.tesol.org/

Conferences and workshops

Association for Business Communication:

http://www.businesscommunication.org/

Association Internationale de Linguistique Appliquée (AILA) World Congress:

http://www.aila.info

American Association of Applied Linguistics (AAAL) annual conference:

http://www.aaal.org

European Society for the Study of English:

http://www.essenglish.org/

TESOL:

http://www.tesol.org

Corpora

The following is a list of corpora that include, or completely consist of, samples of authentic Business English (spoken and/or written). A number of studies featured in this volume are based on Business English material taken from one or more of these corpora.

Open American National Corpus (ANC):

http://www.anc.org/

Bank of English (BoE):

http://www.titania.bham.ac.uk/docs/svenguide.html

British National Corpus (BNC):

http://www.natcorp.ox.ac.uk/

Cambridge English corpus and Cambridge and Nottingham Business English Corpus (CANBEC):

http://www.cambridge.org/us/cambridgeenglish/about-cambridge-english/cambridge-english-corpus

Corpus of Contemporary American English (COCA):

http://corpus.byu.edu/coca/

Hong Kong Corpus of Spoken English (HKCSE):

http://rcpce.engl.polyu.edu.hk/HKCSE/

International Corpus of English (ICE):

http://www.ucl.ac.uk/english-usage/projects/ice.htm

Macmillan World English Corpus:

http://www.macmillandictionary.com/about.html

Oxford corpus:

http://www.oxforddictionaries.com/words/the-oxford-english-corpus

Wordbanks online (Collins):

http://www.collins.co.uk/page/Wordbanks+Online

Online teaching resources

The following are online sources of information that could be useful to Business English teachers and materials designers.

#ELTChat session summary: How can you teach Business English with minimal experience of being in the business world?:

http://theteacherjames.blogspot.nl/2011/10/eltchat-summary-by-edith-occelli-how.html

English for the workplace blog:

http://englishfortheworkplace.blogspot.com/

English language teaching global blog:

http://oupeltglobalblog.com/category/business-english-for-specific-purposes/

TESOL blog:

http://blog.tesol.org/category/blog/

References

Akar, D. (2002). The macro contextual factors shaping business discourse: The Turkish case. *International Review of Applied Linguistics in Language Teaching*, 40(4), 305–22.

Akar, D., & Louhiala-Salminen, L. (1999). Towards a new genre: A comparative study of business faxes. In F. Bargiela-Chiappini & C. Nickerson, (Eds.), *Writing business: Genres, media and discourses* (pp. 227–54). Harlow: Longman.

Austin, J. L. (1962). *How to do things with words*. London: Oxford University Press.

Bargiela-Chiappini, F., & Harris, S. (1997). *Managing language: The discourse of corporate meetings*. Amsterdam & Philadelphia: John Benjamins.

Bargiela-Chiappini, F., Nickerson, C., & Planken, B. (2013). *Business discourse*. Basingstoke: Palgrave Macmillan.

Baxter, R., Boswood, T., & Peirson-Smith, A. (2002). An ESP program for management in the horse-racing business. In T. Orr (Ed.), *English for specific purposes* (pp. 117–46). Alexandria, VA: TESOL, Inc.

Bhatia, V. K. (1993). *Analysing genre: Language in professional settings*. London: Longman.

——(2002). Professional discourse: Towards a multi-dimensional approach and shared practice. In C. Candlin (Ed.), *Research and practice in professional discourse* (pp. 39–60). Hong Kong: City University of Hong Kong Press.

——(2004). *Worlds of written discourse. A genre-based view*. London: Continuum.

Bhatia, V. (2008). Genre analysis, ESP and professional practice. *English for Specific Purposes*, 27(2), 161–74.

Bhatia, V. K. (2010). Interdiscursivity in professional communication. *Discourse & Communication*, 4(1), 32–50.

Bhatia, V. K., & Bremner, S. (2012). English for business communication. *Language Teaching*, 45(4), 410–45.

Bhatia, V. K., & Candlin, C. N. (Eds.) (2001). *Teaching English to meet the needs of business education in Hong Kong*. Hong Kong: City University of Hong Kong.

Blattner, G., & Lomicka, L. (2012). Facebook-ing and the social generation: A new era of language learning. *Alsic, 15*(1). Retrieved October 4, 2014, from http://alsic.revues.org/2413.

Blicq, R., & Moretto, L. A. (1998). *Technically – write! Communicating in a technological era* (6th ed.). Engelwood Cliffs, NJ: Prentice Hall.

Boden, D. (1994). *The business of talk: Organizations in action*. Cambridge: Polity Press.

Bremner, S. (2008). Intertextuality and business communication textbooks: Why students need more textual support. *English for Specific Purposes*, 27(3), 306–21.

——(2010). Collaborative writing: Bridging the gap between the textbook and the workplace. *English for Specific Purposes, 29*(2), 121–32.

Brett, P. (2000). Integrating multimedia into the Business English curriculum: A case study. *English for Specific Purposes, 19*(3), 269–90.

Brown, J. D. (2006). Second language studies: Curriculum development. In K. Brown (Ed.), *Encyclopaedia of language and linguistics*, volume 11 (pp. 102–110). Oxford: Elsevier.

Brown, P., & Levinson, S. (1987). *Politeness.* Cambridge: Cambridge University Press.

Brown, T. P., & Lewis, M. (2002). An ESP project: Analysis of an authentic workplace conversation. *English for Specific Purposes, 22*(1), 93–98.

Capucho, F., & Oliveira, A. M. (2005). EU & I: On the notion of intercomprehension. In A. Martins (Ed.), *Building bridges: EU&I. European awareness and intercomprehension* (pp. 11–18). Viseu: Universidade Cato'lica Portuguesa, Centro Regional das Beiras.

Chan, C. (2009). Forging a link between research and pedagogy: A holistic framework for evaluating business English materials. *English for Specific Purposes, 28*(2), 125–36.

Chan, C., & Frendo, E. (Eds.) (2014). *New ways in teaching business English.* Alexandria, VA: TESOL.

Charles, M. (1996). Business negotiations: Interdependence between discourse and the business relationship. *English for Specific Purposes, 15*(1), 19–36.

Charles, M., & Marschan-Piekkari, R. (2002). Language training for enhanced horizontal communication: A challenge for MNCs. *Business Communication Quarterly, 65*(2), 9–29.

Cheng, W., & Mok, E. (2008). Discourse processes and products: Land surveyors in Hong Kong. *English for Specific Purposes, 27*(1), 57–73.

Chew, S. K. (2005). An investigation of the English language skills used by new entrants in banks in Hong Kong. *English for Specific Purposes, 24*(4), 423–35.

Connor, U., Davis, K., & De Rycker, T. (1995). Correctness and clarity in applying for overseas jobs: A cross-cultural analysis of US and Flemish applications. *Text, 15*(4), 457–76.

Connor, U., Davis, K., De Rycker, T., Phillips, E. M., & Verkens, J. P. (1997). An international course in international business writing: Belgium, Finland, the United States. *Business Communication Quarterly, 60*(4), 63–74.

Devitt, A. J. (1991). Intertextuality in tax accounting: Generic, referential and functional. In C. Bazerman & J. Paradis (Eds.), *Textual dynamics of the professions: Historical and contemporary studies of writing in professional communities* (pp. 336–57). Madison, WI: University of Wisconsin Press.

Douglas, D. (2013). ESP and assessment. In B. Paltridge & S. Starfield (Eds.), *The handbook of English for specific purposes* (pp. 367–83). Oxford: Wiley-Blackwell.

Dow, E. (1999). Negotiation comes of age: research in non-native contexts and implications for today's business English materials. In M. Hewings & C. Nickerson (Eds.), *Business English: Research into practice* (pp. 83–99). London: Longman.

Drew, P., & Heritage, J. (1992). *Talk at work.* Cambridge: Cambridge University Press.

Dudley-Evans, T. (2001). Team teaching in ESP. In J. Flowerdew & M. Peacock (Eds.), *Research perspectives in English for academic purposes* (pp. 225–38). Cambridge: Cambridge University Press.

Economidou-Kogetsidis, M. (2005). "Yes, tell me please, what time is the midday flight from Athens arriving?": Telephone service encounters and politeness. *Intercultural Pragmatics, 2*(3), 253–73.

Ehlich, K., & Wagner, J. (1995). *The discourse of international negotiations*. Berlin: Mouton de Gruyter.

Esteban, A., & Pérez Cañado, M. (2004). Making the case method work in teaching Business English: A case study. *English for Specific Purposes, 23*(2), 137–61.

Evans, S. (2010). Business as usual: The use of English in the professional world in Hong Kong. *English for Specific Purposes, 29*(3), 153–67.

——(2012). Designing email tasks for the Business English classroom: Implications from a study of Hong Kong's key industries. *English for Specific Purposes, 31*(3), 202–12.

——(2013). "Just wanna give you guys a bit of an update": Insider perspectives on business presentations in Hong Kong. *English for Specific Business Purposes, 32*(4), 195–207.

Firth, A. (Ed.). (1995). *The discourse of negotiation. Studies of language in the workplace*. Oxford: Pergamon.

Firth, A. (1996). The discursive accomplishment of normality: On "lingua franca" English and conversation analysis. *Journal of Pragmatics, 26*(2), 237–59.

Flowerdew, J. (2011). Reconciling contrasting approaches to genre analysis: The whole can equal more than the sum of the parts. In D. Belcher, A. Johns & B. Paltridge (Eds.), *New directions in English for specific purposes research* (pp. 119–45). Michigan: Michigan University Press.

Flowerdew, J., & Wan, A. (2006). Genre analysis of tax computation letters: How and why tax accountants write the way they do. *English for Specific Purposes, 25*(2), 133–53.

——(2010). The linguistic and the contextual in applied genre analysis: The case of the company audit report. *English for Specific Purposes, 29*(2), 78–93.

Flowerdew, L. (2013). Needs analysis and curriculum development in ESP. In B. Paltridge & S. Starfield (Eds.), *The handbook of English for specific purposes* (pp. 325–46). Oxford: Wiley-Blackwell.

Fraser, L., Harich, K., Norby, J., Brzovic, K., Rizkallah, T., & Loewy, D. (2005). Diagnostic and value-added assessment of writing. *Business Communication Quarterly, 68*(3), 290–305.

Friginal, E. (2013). Evaluation of oral performance in outsourced call centres: An exploratory case study. *English for Specific Purposes, 32*(1), 25–35.

Fuertes-Olivera, P., & Gómez-Martínez, S. (2004). Empirical assessment of some learning factors affecting Spanish students of business English. *English for Specific Purposes, 23*(2), 163–80.

Gains, J. (1999). Electronic mail: A new style of communication or just a new medium? An investigation into the text features of e-mail. *English for Specific Purposes, 18*(1), 81–101.

Geertz, C. (1973). Thick description: Toward an interpretive theory of culture. In *The interpretation of cultures: Selected essays* (pp. 3–30). New York: Basic Books.

Gimenez, J. (2000). Business e-mail communication: some emerging tendencies in register. *English for Specific Purposes, 19*(3), 237–51.

——(2002). New media and conflicting realities in multinational corporate communication: A case study. *International Review of Applied Linguistics in Language Teaching, 40*(4), 323–44.

——(2006). Embedded business emails: Meeting new demands in international business communication. *English for Specific Purposes, 25*(2), 154–72.

——(2009). Mediated communication. In F. Bargiela-Chiappini (Ed.), *The Handbook of business discourse* (pp. 132–41). Edinburgh: Edinburgh University Press.

——(2014). Multi-communication and the business English class: Research meets pedagogy. *English for Specific Purposes, 35*, 1–16.

Graddol, D. (2006). *English next*. London: British Council.

de Groot, E. B., Korzilius, H. P. L. M., Gerritsen, M., & Nickerson, C. (2011). There's no place like home: UK-based financial analysts' response to Dutch-English and British-English annual report texts. *IEEE Transactions on Professional Communication, 54*(1), 1–17.

de Groot, E., Korzilius, H., Nickerson C., & Gerritsen, M. (2006). A corpus analysis of text themes and photographic themes in managerial forewords of Dutch-English and British annual general reports. *IEEE Transactions on Professional Communication, 49*(3), 217–35.

Handford, M. (2010). *The language of business meetings*. Cambridge: Cambridge University Press.

Harrison, C. (2003). Visual social semiotics: Understanding how still images make meaning. *Technical Communication, 50*(1), 46–60.

Hill, P., & Zyl, S. van (2002). English and multilingualism in the South African engineering workplace. *World Englishes, 21*(1), 23–35.

Holmes, J. (2000). Victoria University's Language in the Workplace Project: An overview. *Language in the Workplace Occasional Papers, 1*. Retrieved 17 December 2014, from http://www.vuw.ac.nz/lals/lwp.

Holmes, J., & Stubbe, M. (2003). *Power and politeness in the workplace*. Upper Saddle River, NJ: Pearson Education.

Hornikx, J., Van Meurs, F., & De Boer, A. (2010). English or a local language in advertising? The appreciation of easy and difficult English slogans in the Netherlands. *Journal of Business Communication, 47*(2), 169–88.

Huhta, M., Vogt, K., Johnson, E., Tulkki, H., & Hall, D. (2013). *Needs analysis for language course design. A holistic approach to ESP*. Cambridge: Cambridge University Press.

Jackson, J. (2005). An inter-university, cross-disciplinary analysis of business education: Perceptions of business faculty in Hong Kong. *English for Specific Purposes, 24*(3), 293–306.

Johns, A. M. (1980). Cohesion in written business discourse. Some contrasts. *The ESP Journal, 1*(1), 35–44.

Jones, A. & Sin, S. (2012). Achieving professional trustworthiness: Communicative expertise and identity work in professional accounting practice. In C. Candlin & J. Crichton (Eds.), *Discourses of trust* (pp. 151–66). Basingstoke: Palgrave Macmillan.

Jones, C. (2011). Written and computer-mediated communication skills: An employer perspective. *Business Communication Quarterly, 74*(3), 247–70.

Kachru, B. B. (2005). *Asian Englishes: Beyond the canon*. Hong Kong: Hong Kong University Press.

Kankaanranta, A., & Louhiala-Salminen, L. (2010). English? – Oh, it's just work!": A study of BELF users' perceptions. *English for Specific Purposes, 29*(3), 204–9.

Kankaanranta, A., & Planken, B. (2010). BELF competence as business knowledge of internationally operating business professionals. *Journal of Business Communication, 47*(4), 380–407.

Kassim, H., & Ali, F. (2010). English communicative events and skills needed at the workplace: Feedback from the industry. *English for Specific Purposes, 29*, 168–82.

Koester, A. (2002). The performance of speech acts in workplace conversations and the teaching of communicative functions. *System, 30*(2), 167–84.

——(2004). *The language of work*. London & New York: Routledge.

——(2006). *Investigating workplace discourse*. London: Routledge.

——(2012). *Workplace discourse*. London: Continuum.

——(2014). "We'd be prepared to do something, like if you say ... " hypothetical reported speech in business negotiations. *English for Specific Purposes, 36*, 35–46.

Koester, A., & Handford, M. (2013). *Hypothetical reported speech in workplace talk.* Unpublished manuscript.

Koester, A., Pitt, A., Handford, M., & Lisboa, M. (2012). *Business advantage: Theory, practice, skills (Intermediate level)*. Cambridge: Cambridge University Press.

Lam, P., Cheng, W., & Kong, K. (2014). Learning English through workplace communication: An evaluation of existing resources in Hong Kong. *English for Specific Purposes, 34*, 68–78.

Lees, G. (1983). *Negotiate in English*. Walton on Thames: Thomas Nelson.

Li So-mui, F., & Mead, K. (2000). An analysis of English in the workplace: The communication needs of textile and clothing merchandisers. *English for Specific Purposes, 19*(4), 351–68.

Lockwood (2012). Developing an English for specific purposes curriculum for Asian call centres: How theory can inform practice. *English for Specific Purposes, 31*(1), 14–24.

Louhiala-Salminen, L. (1997). Investigating the genre of a business fax: A Finnish case study. *The Journal of Business Communication, 34*(3), 316–33.

——(2002). The fly's perspective: Discourse in the daily routine of a business manager. *English for Specific Purposes, 21*(3), 211–31.

Louhiala-Salminen, L., Charles, M., & Kankaanranta, A. (2005). English as a lingua franca in Nordic corporate mergers: Two case companies. *English for Specific Purposes, 24*(4), 401–21.

Louhiala-Salminen, L., & Kankaanranta, A. (2011). Professional communication in a global business context: the notion of global communicative competence. *IEEE Transactions on Professional Communication, 54*(3), 244–62.

Maier, P. (1992). Politeness strategies in business letters by native and non-native English speakers. *English for Specific Purposes, 11*(3), 189–205.

Morkes, J., & Nielsen, J. (1997). Concise, scannnable and objective: How to write for the web. Retrieved October 1, 2014, from http://www.nngroup.com/articles/concise-scannable-and-objective-how-to-write-for-the-web/.

Nelson, M. (2000). Mike Nelson's business English lexis site. Retrieved December 11, 2014, from http://users.utu.fi/micnel/business_english_lexis_site.htm.

——(2006). Semantic associations in Business English: A corpus-based analysis. *English for Specific Purposes, 25*(2), 217–34.

Nickerson, C. (1999). The use of English in electronic mail in a multinational corporation. In F. Bargiela-Chiappini & C. Nickerson (Eds.), *Writing business: Genres, media and discourses* (pp. 35–56). Harlow: Longman.

——(2000). *Playing the corporate language game. An investigation of the genres and discourse strategies in English used by Dutch writers working in multinational corporations*. Amsterdam & Atlanta: Rodopi.

——(2005). English as a lingua franca in international business contexts. *English for Specific Purposes, 24*(4), 367–80.

———(2009). The challenge of the multilingual workplace. In L. Louhiala-Salminen & A. Kankaanranta (Eds.), *The ascent of international business communication* (pp. 193–204). Helsinki: Helsinki School of Economics.

———(2015). Unity in diversity: The view from the (UAE) classroom. *Language Teaching, 48*(2), 235–49.

Nickerson, C., Gerritsen, M., & Meurs, F. van (2005). Raising student awareness of the use of English for specific business purposes in the European context: A staff–student project. *English for Specific Purposes, 24*(3), 333–46.

Nickerson, C., & Goby, V. P. (2014). Accreditation and assessment of learning in the UAE. *Quality Assurance in Education, 22*(3), 212–25.

Northcott, J., & Brown, G. (2006). Legal translator training: Partnership between teachers of English for legal purposes and legal specialists. *English for Specific Purposes 25*(3), 358–75.

O'Sullivan, B. (2006). *Issues in testing business English: The revision of the Cambridge business English certificates.* Cambridge: Cambridge University Press.

Paltridge, B. (2013). Genre and English for specific purposes. In B. Paltridge & S. Starfield (Eds.), *The handbook of English for specific purposes* (pp. 347–66). Oxford: Wiley-Blackwell.

Planken, B. (2005). Managing rapport in lingua franca sales negotiations: A comparison of professional and aspiring negotiators. *English for Specific Purposes, 24*(4), 381–400.

Planken, B., Hooft, A. van, & Korzilius, H. (2004). Promoting intercultural communication competence through foreign language courses. *Business Communication Quarterly, 67*(3), 308–15.

Planken, B., & Kreps, A. (2006). Raising students' awareness of the implications of multimodality for content design and usability: The website project. *Business Communication Quarterly, 69*(4), 421–52.

Planken, B., Meurs, W. F. J. van, & Radlinska, A. (2010). The effects of the use of English in Polish product advertisements: Implications for English for business purposes. *English for Specific Purposes, 29*(4), 225–42.

Poncini, G. (2002). Investigating discourse in business meetings with multicultural participation. *IRAL, 40*(4), 345–73.

———(2004). *Discursive strategies in multicultural business meetings.* Bern: Peter Lang.

Randall, M., & Samimi, M.A. (2010). The status of English in Dubai. *English Today, 26*(1), 43–50.

Rapanta, C., Nickerson, C., & Goby, V. (2014). "Going mobile" in business communication at an Arabian Gulf University. *Business and Professional Communication Quarterly, 77*(4), 357–75.

Rogerson-Revell, P. (2007). Using English for International Business: a European case study. *English for Specific Purposes, 26*(1), 103–20.

———(2008). Participation and performance in international business meetings. *English for Specific Purposes, 27*(3), 338–60.

———(2010). Can you spell that for us non-native speakers? Accommodation strategies in international business meetings. *Journal of Business Communication, 47*(4), 432–54.

Schegloff, E. & Sacks, H. (1973). Openings and closings. *Semiotica, 8*(4), 289–327.

Schullery, N. (1999). Selecting workable cases for classroom use. *Business Communication Quarterly, 62*(4), 77–80.

Seshadri, S., & Theye, L. (2000). Professionals and professors: Substance or style? *Business Communication Quarterly, 63*(3), 9–23.

Sims, B. R. & Guice, S. (1992). Differences between business letters from native and non-native speakers of English. *The Journal of Business Communication, 29*(1), 23–39.

Sin, S. (2011). *An investigation of practitioners' and students' conceptions of accounting work.* Linkoping: Linkoping University Press.

Sin, S., Jones, A., & Petocz, P. (2007). Evaluating a method of integrating generic skills with accounting content based on a functional theory of meaning. *Accounting and Finance, 47*(1), 143–63.

Sin, S., Reid, A., & Jones, A. (2012). An exploration of students' conceptions of accounting work. *Accounting Education: An International Journal, 21*(4), 323–40.

Spencer-Oatey, H. (2000). Rapport management: A framework for analysis. In H. Spencer-Oatey (Ed.), *Culturally speaking: Managing rapport through talk across cultures* (pp. 11–46). London: Continuum.

Spyridakis, J. H. (2000). Guidelines for authoring comprehensible web pages and evaluating their success. *Technical Communication, 47*(3), 359–82.

St John, M. J. (1996). Business is booming: Business English in the 1990s. *English for Specific Purposes, 15*(1), 3–18.

Stoller, F. (2006). Establishing a theoretical foundation for project-based learning in second and foreign-language contexts. In G. H. Beckett & P. C. Miller (Eds.), *Project-based second and foreign language education: Past, present, and future* (pp.19–40). Greenwich, Connecticut: Information Age Publishing.

Swales, J. M. (1990). *Genre analysis.* Cambridge: Cambridge University Press.

Swales, J. M., & Feak, C. (1995). *Academic writing for graduate students.* Ann Arbor: The University of Michigan Press.

Tardy, C. M. (2009). *Building genre knowledge.* West Lafayette, IN: Parlor Press.

Tovey, J. (1998). Organizing features of hypertext: Some rhetorical and practical elements. *Journal of Business and Technical Communication, 12*(3), 371–80.

Trinder, R. (2013). Business students' beliefs about language learning in a university context. *English for Specific Purposes, 32*(1), 1–11.

Turner, T., Qvarfordt, P., Biehl, J., Golovchinsky, G., & Back, M. (2010). Exploring the workplace communication ecology. In *CHI '10: Proceedings of the 28th international conference on Human factors in computing systems* (pp. 841–50). New York: ACM.

U.S. Department of Health and Human Services (n.d.). Research-based web design and usability guidelines. Retrieved October 1, 2014, from http://www.usability.gov/sites/default/files/documents/guidelines_book.pdf?post=yes.

Walker, C. (2011). How a corpus-based study of the factors which influence collocation can help in the teaching of business English. *English for Specific Purposes, 30*(2), 101–12.

Warren, M. (2013). "*Just spoke to ...* ": The types and directionality of intertextuality in professional discourse. *English for Specific Purposes, 32*(1), 12–24.

Williams, M. (1988). Language taught for meetings and language used in meetings: Is there anything in common? *Applied Linguistics, 9*(1), 45–58.

Zhang, Z. (2007). Towards an integrated approach to teaching Business English: A Chinese experience. *English for Specific Purposes, 26*(4), 399–410.

——(2013). Business English students learning to write for international business: What do international business practitioners have to say about their texts? *English for Specific Purposes, 32*(3), 144–56.

Index

accommodation: definition of 16; study of accommodation strategies 48–50; in teaching 50–51

application letters 67–8, 96; across cultures 68, 73–4; moves in 68, 159

assessment 8, 157–8; assessment framework 9; curriculum assessment 11; lingua franca model 40; native speaker norm 24

authentic language 48, 149, 151; discrepancy with business English teaching materials 4–5, 7, 29, 30, 154–6; importance of 30–1

awareness-raising tasks: spoken business English 37, 44, 50, 57, 60–1; written business English 74, 75, 82, 83, 85, 126; intertextuality 111; different media 117, 126, 136

BELF 12, 21, 24, 159; analysis of 19–21; definition of 15, 16, 20; in context 21–4; teaching of 17–19

business English: around the world 10–11; characteristics of 12, 19–20, 38, 72; competence 20–1, 40; definition of 3; lexis 29, 32, 42–3, 68, 71, 150–1; versus English for Specific Purposes 5–6

business letters: structure of 67–8, 73

business letters, studies of 10, 67–8, 73, 77–9, 90, 92, 96–7, 159

business meetings: developing materials for; 152–4; language of 5, 30, 58–60; structure of 32, 33

business meetings, studies of 10, 32–4, 41–4, 48–50, 58–60, 74, 149

business talk: definition of 28–9; versus everyday talk 28–30

collaborative writing: audit reports 78–9; committee papers 80–1; Hong Kong Jockey Club study 80–1; in teaching materials 154–5; tax computation letters 77–8

communicative purpose: analysis of 52, 66–8, 70, 71, 74

computer-mediated communication: in the classroom 94–6, 116–17, 122–9, 140–2; skills required by employees 121; studies of 88–90, 92–4

contextual factors 34–5; business culture 32, 69–72, 75; business relationship 42, 47, 48, 59, 72; experience 46–7, 54–7, 73, 96; in the classroom 88–96; national culture 69–70, 73–4; power difference 28–9, 60, 156; roles 29, 34–5, 36, 42–3; social distance 29, 33, 60, 156

conversation analysis 32, 38, 54, 149

corpora of English: ABOT 31, 53, 60; BEC 29; BNC 29, 151, 162; CANBEC 31, 53, 58, 149, 150, 162; Indianapolis Business Learner Corpus 72, 73; Language in the Workplace Project 11, 31, 33

corpus-based research 31, 149–52, 153, 154

developing teaching materials from research: analysis of existing textbook materials 152–7; communication audits 8–9, 15, 146–9; corpus-based studies 149–52, 153, 154; needs analysis surveys 6–9, 17–19, 80–1, 139, 146–9, 153

discourse analysis 38, 39, 54

discourse-based studies 38, 53, 60; of spoken business English 31–8